PRINCIPLES
OF
DEPRECIATION

This is a volume in the
Arno Press collection

DIMENSIONS OF ACCOUNTING
THEORY AND PRACTICE

Advisory Editor
Richard P. Brief

See last pages of this volume
for a complete list of titles

PRINCIPLES

OF

DEPRECIATION

EARL A. SALIERS

ARNO PRESS

A New York Times Company

New York • 1980

Editorial Supervision: Brian Quinn

Reprint Edition 1980 by Arno Press Inc.
Reprinted from a copy in the University of Illinois Library

DIMENSIONS OF ACCOUNTING THEORY AND PRACTICE
ISBN for complete set: 0-405-13475-4
See last pages of this volume for titles.

Manufactured in the United States of America

Library of Congress Cataloging in Publication Data

Saliers, Earl Adolphus, 1884-
Principles of depreciation.

(Dimensions of accounting theory and practice)
Reprint of the 1916 ed. published by Ronald Press Co., New York, in series: Ronald accounting series.
Bibliography: p.
Includes index.
1. Depreciation. I. Title. II. Series. III. Series: Ronald accounting series.
HF5681.D5S3 1980 657'.73 80-1576
ISBN 0-405-13542-4

PRINCIPLES
OF
DEPRECIATION

BY

EARL A. SALIERS, Ph.D.

Assistant Professor of Accounting, Sheffield Scientific School of Yale University

(Second Printing)

RONALD ACCOUNTING SERIES

NEW YORK
THE RONALD PRESS COMPANY
1916

William G. Hewitt Press, Brooklyn, Printers
J. F. Tapley Co., New York, Binders

To my Father and Mother

this book is most affectionately dedicated in appreciation of their steadfast interest in my work

PREFACE

The general subject of depreciation has recently been given much attention by accountants, engineers, and others interested in the financial and mechanical problems of modern corporate enterprise. Vast accumulations of wealth and a great range in the possibilities of investment have necessitated a study of the economics of business with a view to increased efficiency, safety, and justice in the complex field of industry.

In this book a study is made of the depreciation of capital values which in their manifold forms constitute a large share of the world's wealth. Oftentimes regarded as an abstract and theoretical problem, it is really one of intense practicability. In the nature of things it is an unavoidable problem, and any objection that may be offered on the score of its indefiniteness is outweighed by the necessity of mastering it.

The depreciation problem may be viewed from two standpoints—that of the accountant and that of the engineer. The engineer deals with physical conditions, studies plant deterioration, the necessity of replacement, and so on. The accountant devises ways and means of recording in the most intelligible manner the facts in connection with these changes. The work of the two should be correlated through a common understanding of the character and extent of depreciation. The engineer having shown what the rate of depreciation is, the accountant suggests devices for recording it, for providing replacement funds, etc., and thus for the preservation of capital value.

Various methods have been suggested as suitable for determining the annual depreciation charge. Some of these require computations involving the use of algebraic formulas. These formulas are explained fully, and illustrated by the solution of problems and also by the use of graphic charts. It is thought best to use twenty-five years as a period sufficiently long to indicate clearly the effect of interest on the calculations, and at the same time not too long to be extraordinary.

Much literature on valuations has recently appeared, and while no pretense is made at giving an exhaustive consideration of that subject, it is believed that in so far as depreciation is a factor in valuations a tolerably complete discussion of it is presented here, due allowance being made for the somewhat unsettled condition of the whole subject.

The past decade has witnessed a remarkable extension of governmental supervision of industry. An attempt is made to give this phase of the matter the consideration which its importance warrants. The legislatures through their laws, and the courts through their decisions, exert a great influence—not always consistent perhaps—in the financing and managing of business enterprise. For example, the recently enacted income tax law makes it quite necessary for business men to study the depreciation question carefully in order to report intelligently to the Government. While much space is given to this new phase of the situation, this is justified by the suddenness with which we have been brought face to face with it, and by the prospect of its future permanence.

EARL A. SALIERS

Lehigh University,
May 1, 1915.

CONTENTS

PART I—THEORY

APPENDIX

FORMS

Principles of Depreciation

Part I—Theory

CHAPTER I

CHARACTER OF INDUSTRIAL PLANT

Twofold Character of Capital

Modern methods of production and distribution require the investment of large amounts of capital in the form of fixed assets. This may be seen by a glance at any undertaking of an industrial nature. Thus a factory is composed of the site, the buildings, and the equipment of machinery and tools. Land, ballasted roadbeds, ties, rails, rolling stocks, station houses, etc., are the elements which enter into the material equipment of a railroad company. Capital so invested constitutes one of the great divisions of wealth, and may be distinguished from another form of wealth known as circulating capital, which finds representation in current assets, such as cash and merchandise. The subject matter of this book is confined entirely to a consideration of capital invested in the form of fixed assets.

Corporate Organization

Much of the world's wealth is piloted through productive channels by the agency of corporate organization. Corporations may now be regarded as guardians of the people's wealth, and presumably are financed and managed in the interest of the stockholders, the creditors, and the public. That the general public, or the consumers, have in many instances a very direct interest in the corporate organizations by which they are served, is now fully recognized.

When the corporation is formed, funds are secured by assessments upon the stockholders or by the sale of securities, or by both, and these are expended in the purchase of the properties—tangible and intangible—required in the particular industry. Although the stockholders and the bondholders continue to be the owners of this invested wealth, the control of it passes to a great degree into the hands of a board of directors and other corporate officials.

Corporations Concentrate Wealth

A few responsible men thus acquire control of a large amount of wealth, representing harvests gleaned from wide fields. Subjects of many nations are sometimes stockholders of the same corporations. In this way wealth is concentrated where it is most effective. Promoters and organizers have this in view. The promoter interests the investor, secures his good will and his money, and, with the latter, assets needed in the projected business are purchased or constructed.

Constituents of Plant Value

The economic status of a beginning corporation is somewhat more difficult to comprehend than that of an older one. For a time it exists by consuming a part of its own capital, while normally the cost of existing is met out of the corporation's income. So the investment represents more than the bare cost of the units of which the industrial plant is constituted. There is an additional increment of value which may be regarded as arising from the peculiar adaptability of the various plant units when considered in their relation to one another, and thus as a part of the physical value of the plant; or, as some prefer, it may be regarded as an intangible value. It results from the various preliminary and incidental costs of construction—surveys, legal aid, insurance, taxes, interest on capital, alterations of plans, and so on. Ordinarily such expenditures are charged to revenue, but, during construction, as well as for a time thereafter known as the educational period, they represent proper charges to capital.

Omitting details, an industrial plant may be described as of a threefold character, consisting of:

1. Plant, therein being included all direct costs, as real estate, right of way, etc., with a percentage added for engineering.
2. Equipment, a direct cost to which nothing need be added for overhead except possibly a small percentage for installation.
3. Capitalized general expenditures, including legal services, insurance, taxes, etc., incurred during construction and usually for a time thereafter.

The capitalized general expenditures are in the nature of indirect or overhead costs, and if not known are usually estimated as a percentage on cost of construction of plant and equipment.

Direct Costs

As far as possible all costs of plant and equipment should be charged to the account representing that particular unit of plant in question. Consequently, as already suggested, a certain amount over and above prime cost will be included in the account. In this way all costs are accounted for, except those of a general character, which cannot be charged directly to any particular account, being incident rather to the plant as a whole.

Indirect Costs in Valuations

In valuing public utility properties it is usually necessary to make reproduction cost the basis of the valuation. The prices of the plant units must then be based on prime cost, to which must be added percentages for overhead or indirect costs. The prime cost of the plant is but a part of the actual reproduction cost, because it includes the direct cost only, and does not include indirect cost. Courts and commissions are apt to underestimate this indirect element of cost. Errors and accidents are contingencies sure to occur, but after the occasion has passed they are often ignored because not evident. Nevertheless they are a part of the investment.

Recognition of Indirect Costs by Interstate Commerce Commission

The Interstate Commerce Commission in its classification of expenditures for road and equipment, recognizes the validity of such incidental costs. It provides an account for "Other Expenditures," to which it allows charges for organization expenses, including: cost of printing stocks and bond certificates, cost of disposing of securities, salaries of general officers during the period of construction and of clerks engaged on construction accounting, rent and repair of general offices, office expenses, and such items of an incidental or special character as cannot be charged to any other account.[1]

In the following pages an analysis will be made of the principal indirect costs of industrial plant. An understanding of them is essential to the determination of plant value, and consequently to a thorough understanding of the principles involved in the solution of the depreciation problem.

[1] Classification of Expenditures for Road and Equipment, page 27.

Engineering

This division of cost varies widely in different enterprises as well as in different localities. It is low where an inferior grade of talent can be employed, and high where the best grade of service is demanded. In case of railroads it is usually in the neighborhood of 5% of the cost of construction. This was the percentage used in the recent valuation of the Lehigh Valley Railroad. It must be remembered that the term construction cost, as here used, does not include cost of land for roadbed or other purposes. This accords with the requirements of the Interstate Commerce Commission, as indicated in primary accounts 2 and 3 of their classification of expenditures for road and equipment.

Engineering costs comprise the salaries of engineers and assistants, and their traveling expenses while on duty; also the cost of the various instruments used—transits, tape lines, etc. Of an investment of $26,736,000 in the Metropolitan Water Works, Boston, 7.77% represented engineering expenses, preliminary and constructional. Of the disbursements on the New York water works to the end of September, 1913, 9.78% of the total, or $10,050,000, was for engineering; but costs of extensive boring and investigations were here included which were not included in the Metropolitan Water Works. In the Boston subways the engineering cost ranged from 5.05 to 9.88% of the total cost in different divisions (1895-1912); in the Kennebec New Gravity Water Supply, 6.69% (1906); in the Louisville sewerage works, 9% (1906-1912); in the Springfield, Massachusetts, water works, 10% (1910); and in the Springfield, Massachusetts, Ludlow filters, 17% (1906).

Preliminary Expenses

Before a plant is brought into actual existence, to say

nothing of putting it on a going-concern basis, a more or less extended period transpires during which the work of promoting and financing is being done. Surveys may be required to determine whether a suggested situation is feasible for the proposed plant. Then the consent of the landowners, in the form of options, must be obtained. These and similar activities necessitate the employment of legal, engineering, and financial experts. If the reports warrant it, a charter of incorporation is obtained, securities are offered for sale, the land is acquired, the final surveys are made, and the plans and specifications for the proposed works are completed. If further consideration of the proposed site is not justified by the first researches, it is abandoned for a more promising one; not, however, before considerable money has been spent, which must form a part of the total investment.

Insurance During Construction

This is primary account 45 in the classification of expenditures for road and equipment prescribed by the Interstate Commerce Commission. The cost of insuring property during construction and until the plant is placed on a going-concern basis, should be charged to this account, not as expense, but as investment. During the period of construction a certain amount of property is inevitably destroyed by accident or otherwise, even though due care is used to protect it. For the same reason that insurance is a legitimate expense in a going concern, its cost during construction becomes a part of the investment.

Interest During Construction

This is a large item of cost and deserves careful consideration. The money required must be secured sufficiently in advance of the time when it will be needed, to avoid a possible stringency in the funds with consequent suspension of work and loss. Thus interest must be paid on the money for a considerable time in advance of its disbursement, as well as after, and at a rate somewhat higher than can be had by placing the funds with depositaries until needed. However, to the extent that interest thus received offsets interest paid, to that extent is the total cost reduced.

Interest cost during construction is ordinarily computed as equivalent to the interest on the total cost of construction (not including interest) for one-half the period of construction. This method is based on the assumption that the rate of expenditure remains constant from an investment of zero to an investment of 100%; also that interest is incurred on the money only after it is disbursed. Such an assumption underrates the interest cost, and unless allowance is made for the higher rate of interest demanded for money to be invested in new and speculative enterprises, the actual investment is still further underestimated.

A constant rate of expenditure on plant from the inception to the completion of the work would indeed be exceptional. At times it is greater, and at other times less, than such an assumption implies. During the first half of the period of construction, when most of the materials are purchased, it is usually greater, with a resulting excess of interest cost over that implied by the foregoing theory. Interest during construction is paid out of capital and is as much a part of the investment as cost of machinery or buildings. Consequently interest during construction, just as insurance on buildings, should be capitalized.

Developmental Costs

Some time passes, after construction is completed, before the business reaches a profitable basis. During this period the expenses of an operating concern are incurred, and, owing to the lack of sufficient revenue, must be paid out of capital. This necessitates a larger investment than would otherwise be the case, though not evidenced by any addition to the tangible assets. Investments in construction come largely to a standstill with the beginning of this educational period, but current expenses and interest continue, and add an additional item to the investment. As gross revenue increases, a larger and larger amount of it can be used to meet these obligations, and consequently smaller and smaller charges to capital will be made, until investment on this score ceases altogether.

Of course some limitation must be placed on the developmental period in any case, even though revenues do not increase as anticipated. Capitalization of expenses cannot be indefinitely continued, for the possibility of ever earning a return on the investment would grow more and more remote, and in case of public service corporations would require excessive charges on the service. Some enterprises are by nature losing ventures, and the prolongation of the experimental period and consequent capitalization would constantly widen the chasm between actual income and a satisfactory return on the investment. These principles apply to normal properties. If the venture is a losing one, whether subject to commission control or not, the investor, not the public, must suffer, as is inevitable in the field of open competition.

Investment vs. Income

A thorough knowledge of the items which comprise investment in industrial plant is of increasing importance. Formerly competition was considered the chief agent determining income on investment. It was thought that an investment, whatever its amount or character, receives its equitable reward as the result of the play of competition forces, much as water finds its level by gravitation. But the experiences of the past decade have caused us to alter our notion of the relation of income to investment. Oftentimes competition is quite impossible. Many of our public utility companies receive franchises granting them the right to operate in certain districts to the exclusion of all competitors.

Under such conditions, how may we know whether an adequate return is being received on an investment, unless the amount of the investment itself is carefully calculated? And it is but natural that the next step taken is to regulate the income so that a return may be made adequate to the protection of the investor, and at the same time just to the consumer.

How the Investor is Protected

When the plant enters upon its career of activity, if it is a public service corporation, it is subject to commission regulation, and probably has a monopoly of the market, thus being free from competition of similar concerns. It is directly controlled by a board of directors and other officers. Consumers as well as stockholders and creditors have interests which demand protection. If it is a private corporation, no commission will stand between it and the consumer, but the latter protects himself by bidding in the open market. When the single proprietor directly supervised his own property there was every incentive for him to husband it carefully. Today, however, the control of much wealth is entirely lost to the real owner. But since ownership implies the right of enjoyment and continued possession, the investor must look to the corporation officials, or to a public service commission. They can afford protection by pursuing or enforcing sound financial methods.

Good accounting is based upon the distinction between

capital and revenue. The integrity of all investment rests upon this principle. Unless it is adhered to, investment and income are obscurely merged. As a result, capital is frittered away as dividends and the financial foundations of the company are weakened. The investment must be kept undiminished by providing for its renewal or replacement wherever it leaks away as the result of obsolescence, inadequacy, or decrepitude.

Depreciation

This loss of value, whether tangible or intangible in form, resulting from physical decay, or from obsolescence or inadequacy, which indicate functional decay, is known as depreciation. It necessitates repairs, renewals, and replacements. Did it not occur, every outlay on plant would add to the investment. Depreciation does not result from one cause but from many causes, which sometimes leads to the belief that it cannot be scientifically cared for. But some adequate method of handling it is not merely desirable, but necessary, to a solution of problems arising in the valuation of public utility properties, and in the management of industrial enterprises generally.

Differences in depreciation, not only in unlike properties, but in those of identical construction, frequently occur. A machine constantly exposed to the damaging influence of the elements, even if little used, depreciates rapidly. The same machine adequately sheltered may be operated constantly with but slight deterioration. One machine may be so constructed that ordinary use wears it slowly, and it may become obsolete long before it is worn out. Another deteriorates rapidly in strength, leaving little chance of ever becoming obsolete. Instruments under constant or unusual strain wear rapidly. With a certain amount of experience it is usually possible to forecast with tolerable accuracy the date of physical decrepitude, but it is more difficult to predict possible future obsolescence or inadequacy.

Depreciation Classified

In this book depreciation will be understood to comprehend all losses arising out of physical or functional decay, excepting such as may be compensated for by current repairs. Depreciation may be thought of as affecting the various units composing plant, or as affecting the whole plant. Depreciation may therefore be classified, according to viewpoint, into *unit* depreciation, which is the decay of individual machines or other units of plant, and *composite* depreciation, which is the resultant effect upon the whole plant of *unit* depreciation. Total depreciation of plant is therefore the *composite* depreciation, which is equal to the sum of the *unit* depreciations at any time.

There is this difference, however, between unit and composite depreciation: that whereas unit depreciation gradually increases from zero to approximately 100% of the amount originally invested in the units of plant, composite depreciation increases from zero to a certain percentage of the original investment in the entire plant, say 15 or 20%, beyond which it is prevented from going because of the continuous replacement of wornout or obsolete units of plant; but can never be entirely extinguished, except in the extreme case of complete replacement, because of the greater or less degree of depreciation of the units composing the plant.

Current repairs are not included in depreciation, because, with the exception of the first few years of a plant's life, their cost is spread quite evenly over the accounting periods, and they can be met out of current revenue without affecting the equilibrium of the investment. Any items of so large an amount as to burden the year in which they must be met, cannot, however, be classified as current repairs, but should be provided for under the head of depreciation.

Unit Depreciation

Thus parts of plant must sometimes be renewed which would be an unjust charge upon current revenue. By long use they have lost all their value except what they may be worth as scrap. Machines, as Karl Marx says, are congealed labor. By use this congealed labor has been expended on output which the machine assisted in producing. Or, as P. D. Leake expresses it, the capital outlay on the machine has expired, and to avoid a continual diminution of the capital outlay on the whole plant it must be replaced. When a machine that has been transferring its value into commodities for twenty years, at last collapses, it ought not to be replaced out of current revenue unless the replacements are so numerous that their cost would be evenly distributed from year to year. Not only would this result in an unwonted irregularity in apparent net profits, but to a recent buyer of stock it would mean a charge to replace something from which this stockholder has derived no material benefit.

It is therefore proper to arrange so that the cost of a renewal which will last several years may be equitably charged to revenue during those years, instead of making the entire charge to current revenue. In a very extensive plant composed of many and varied assets, this rule may be ignored, for there renewals are quite the same as current repairs in a smaller plant, and become evenly distributed from year to year. When such is the case it is not improper to charge the entire cost of renewals to current revenue, but it is usually better to differentiate between these two classes of expense.

Composite Depreciation

Even with current repairs and renewals satisfactorily met, the investment value of a new plant will continue to decline to a certain point, unless counterbalanced by the unearned increment in values of land, or strategic location. It is better not to offset the depreciation of wasting assets by the unearned increment, even if there is a certainty of the latter's existence. It may be conservatively omitted from the balance sheet. A large portion of every plant, after the passage of twenty-five years, has exhausted a considerable portion of its useful life, the extent being dependent on the character of the individual units of which the plant is composed. Not all parts can be kept entirely new and undepreciated. Nor, on the other hand, can all parts become worn out or obsolete without destroying the plant's efficiency. During the early years of the plant's life no renewals and but few repairs are needed, and depreciation apparently continues unchecked. When repairs and renewals do become necessary they do not bring the plant back to original value, but merely keep it from becoming even less valuable. On first thought it might appear that diminution of value would continue until normally the plant value, being represented by an average of miscellaneous units in all stages of depreciation, would be approximately 50% of cost new. Since, however, a large part of the investment does not depreciate at all, the reduction in value will probably be found, ordinarily, not to exceed 20 or 25% of original value.

Preventing Overcapitalization

If the outstanding stock is not diminished in amount, the net result of this composite depreciation is overcapitalization, since the assets no longer equal their former value. Such overcapitalization may be prevented in two ways:

Either the capital may be amortized by retiring stock to an amount equal to the fall in values, charging the cost of such retirement to revenue and thus diminishing permanently the capital; or a replacement reserve may be created to offset this unavoidable decline in values, in which case capital may be retained at the old figure.

This replacement reserve may be employed in the purchase of additional assets, when not needed for specific replacements, and still the transaction will be essentially a replacement. Consequently all parts of the plant bought, up to the limit of the reserve, will be divided into two classes: (1) actual replacements, and (2) units which are not actual replacements, being apparently additions, but which are essentially of the character of replacements, because they replace values lost through the partial depreciation of other assets.

As it is customary in making an actual replacement to charge the depreciation reserve with the cost of the item replaced (see Chapter IV), a slight complication arises here, because no specific replacement is made, and it would therefore be impossible to charge the reserve with the cost of any particular unit of plant. The reserve would therefore remain credited with the full amount, and be charged only when a unit is discarded and without regard to the time when the new assets which replace the value of the discarded unit, were purchased.

Of course, if assets are purchased exceeding in value the total accrued depreciation indicated by the reserve, they are, to the extent of the excess, extensions, not replacements. If due allowance is made for depreciation accrued, the distinction between replacements and betterments will work out automatically in the balance sheet. Thus, if the following balance sheet represents the true status of Company A,

BALANCE SHEET OF COMPANY A, AS AT......

Plant	$100,000		Capital Stock Outstanding	$110,000
Less Reserve for Depreciation..	20,000	$80,000		
Cash		30,000		
		$110,000		$110,000

then the following balance sheet shows the situation after an apparent addition, but in reality a replacement, has been made:

BALANCE SHEET OF COMPANY A, AS AT......

Plant	$100,000		Capital Stock Outstanding	$110,000
Less Reserve for Depreciation..	20,000	$80,000		
New Building..........		20,000		
Cash		10,000		
		$110,000		$110,000

The $20,000 paid for the new building is the amount which was charged to gross revenue as depreciation cost when the reserve for depreciation was credited, and represents a return of the investment to the company, that much of the investment having gone out in services or output. Had it been employed to amortize capital instead, the balance sheet would appear thus:

BALANCE SHEET OF COMPANY A, AS AT......

Plant	$100,000		Capital Stock Outstanding	$90,000
Less Reserve for Depreciation..	20,000	$80,000		
Cash		10,000		
		$90,000		$90,000

Had the new building cost $30,000, it would be partly a replacement ($20,000), and partly a betterment ($10,000), since $10,000 of the $30,000 of cash on hand represents original investment, not revenue withheld to compensate for depreciation. The balance sheet would then have appeared as follows, although the amount of the replacement and of the extension might not always be tabulated.

BALANCE SHEET OF COMPANY A, AS AT......

Plant	$100,000		Capital Stock Outstanding	$110,000
Less Reserve for Depreciation..	20,000	$80,000		
New Building:				
Replacement..	$20,000			
Betterment...	10,000	30,000		
		$110,000		$110,000

If formed by equal annual charges, the depreciation reserve will accumulate rapidly while the plant is still new and renewals are few, and should be sufficient to amortize capital, as suggested, or to secure the replacement of decreased asset values by needed improvements. If capital is amortized, the charge necessary to afford a fair income is lessened. In either case the plant's efficiency should actually increase, since, as shown later, efficiency may remain at practically 100% even where there is considerable depreciation; while depreciation makes it possible to extend the plant to a certain extent without increasing the investment.

Functional Depreciation

Viewed from the standpoint of cause of the depreciation rather than from that of its effect on plant units and composite plant, depreciation may be again classified into *functional* and *physical* depreciation. Functional depreciation results from the obsolescence or the inadequacy of a plant unit, or a combination of plant units. A thing is obsolete when it has been rendered entirely valueless as the result of some invention or discovery, and this may occur where it has not depreciated at all physically. A thing is obsolescent when its value is being reduced by inventions or discoveries but has not yet wholly disappeared.

Inadequacy, on the other hand, indicates that a thing is incapable of fully performing the function for which it is intended. It indicates neither physical depreciation nor obsolescence. Inadequacy may result from expansion of markets, community growth, and so on.

The extent to which the service may be cheapened in case of obsolescence, or bettered in case of inadequacy, by the installation of a new plant or unit of plant, determines the amount of the functional depreciation of the old plant or plant unit. It must be written down to such an extent that the production cost of service will be no more for the old than for the new plant.

Obsolescence

If the first cost of the old and the new plants, respectively, be added to the capitalized cost of operating them, the difference, assuming that both perform the same service, represents the depreciation of the old plant from obsolescence.

If the first cost of an old machine was $1,000, and its yearly operating expense is $200; and a new machine which will perform the same total service as the old one will do so at an annual operating expense of $100, and a first cost of $2,200, then if money is worth 5%, the capitalized cost of operation for the old machine is $200 ÷ .05, or $4,000; and for the new machine, $100 ÷ .05, or $2,000. Adding these to the first costs, we have for the old machine:

Original cost	$1,000
Capitalized operating cost	4,000
Total capitalized cost	$5,000

and for the new machine:

Original cost	$2,200
Capitalized operating cost	2,000
Total capitalized cost	$4,200

The value of the old machine has therefore been reduced through obsolescence ($5,000 — $4,200, or $800) to a present value ($1,000 — $800) of $200; $4,200 represents the highest capitalized cost necessary to perform the given service. If a machine could be purchased for $4,200 which would incur no operating expenses, the capitalized cost would be the same as in the case of a machine costing $2,200 and operated for $100 a year, and the old machine would still be worth only $200. If the old machine cost $250 per year to operate, this capitalized ($250 ÷ .05 = $5,000 + $1,000 = $6,000) would exceed the total capitalized cost of running the new machine by $1,800, which would give the old machine a minus value of $800, and a yearly saving of $800 × .05, or $40, would be made by discarding it and purchasing the new one.

Inadequacy

Depreciation due to inadequacy may be found on the above basis, or on the basis of the capitalized cost of production of a unit of output. The latter may be the better basis, especially if more than one old unit of plant is required to do the same work one new one will do. Thus, if the total cost of producing a unit of output by the old machine is $20, and by the new machine $18, the saving per unit is $2. If the number of units of output produced annually by the old machine is 100, then the total annual saving is \$200. \$200 ÷ .05 = \$4,000, which sum represents functional depreciation of the old plant and the amount over and above the depreciated value of the old plant which the company can afford to pay for a new machine, providing the old one can be disposed of at its depreciated value.

Effective Depreciation

Whichever kind of depreciation—physical or functional—is the greater, that one is the effective one in determining unit depreciation. The lesser one is ineffective and should not be added to the greater. Some units of a plant will be influenced more by functional and others more by physical depreciation, while the extent of depreciation of the entire plant, or composite depreciation, will be the resultant of both as they operate upon the plant units. Total composite depreciation may therefore be more largely the resultant of physical or of functional depreciation, depending upon which affects more extensively the units of the plant. It would rarely be made up entirely of one to the exclusion of the other.

Depreciation of Indirect Costs

We have seen that into every plant there must enter certain costs of an indirect character, a part of which may be apportioned directly to the units of plant, but the remainder of which, being of a general character incident rather to the plant as a whole, must be charged to some capital account such as General Expenditures. If these values depreciate along with the material assets, allowance must be made for them. On the other hand, if the benefits derived from them are of a permanent character they need not be written down. Some of these costs are purely incidental to the constructional and educational periods and ordinarily will not be incurred again. The costs of preliminary surveys and engineering, and of at least a part of the policing and contingencies during construction and development, will remain largely or wholly non-depreciating, except in case of mines and similar properties of limited lifetime. Interest, taxes, and insurance during construction become a part of the permanent investment if not again incurred.

Proportion of Overhead to Direct Costs

These overhead charges constitute a large part of the investment, ranging from 20 to 40% or more of prime cost. In the valuation of the Lehigh Valley Railroad they were estimated at 30.74%, and in the Buffalo, Rochester & Eastern at 40.3% of prime cost.

The Knoxville Water Case

Reference should be made to the recent change which has taken place in the attitude of the courts toward companies engaged in various industries, growing out of a better understanding of the character of industrial plant. This change is well reflected in the decision of the Supreme Court of the United States in the Knoxville Water Case.[2] Here the court stated definitely that before any question of profit can be raised, not only current repairs, but replacements and depreciation, must be made good out of earnings. No company must have its properties wasted without adequate provision for replacement. The original investment must not be diminished, and it is the company's duty to security holders and to the public to see that it is not. The only alternative would be the issue of new securities with consequent overcapitalization, followed by disaster to the business.

[2] 212 U. S. 1.

Mining Companies, Leases, Patents

Corporations engaged in mining are exceptions to the rule that the investment must be kept from diminishing. There is good authority both in England[3] and the United States[4] for the distribution of the proceeds of mining operations without making the customary retention for decrease in value of the mines through extraction of minerals. The same principle applies to any concern utilizing a wasting asset—one which can only be made useful by being consumed.

---

[3] Lee *v.* Neuchatel Co., 41 Ch. Div. 1.

[4] People *v.* Roberts, 156 N. Y. 585; see Clark on Corporations, pages 333, 334.

CHAPTER II

ANALYSIS OF A HYDROELECTRIC PLANT

In the preceding chapter the general characteristics of industrial plant were described. In practice the depreciation problem can be adequately handled only by first making an analysis of the units of which such a plant is composed, based upon their use, value, and longevity. In this chapter such an analysis will be made of a hydroelectric plant for the purpose of affording an illustration and to serve as subject matter for further discussion of the question of method in caring for depreciation.

Definition of a Unit

The word "unit," as used in this and the following chapter, will be understood to mean a subdivision of plant, consisting of one, a few, or even many items, as determined by a consideration of use, value, and longevity; the unit in each case being the most suitable portion of plant to employ as a basis for figuring depreciation. Thus a unit may be a building, or twenty locomotives of similar class, or a steamboat, or the hulls of ten similarly constructed steamboats, and so on, the question being always one of expediency and determined upon the actual conditions. The following rules may be of assistance:

1. A unit of plant cannot be made up of unlike things, or things having different functions.

2. For the sake of the saving in calculations, a unit should include as many items as possible capable of being handled together.

3. A number of things may be handled together as a

unit if they have the same general physical make-up, are employed for the same purpose, and, what would be ordinarily inferred from the foregoing, have approximately the same lifetime.

Thus a number of locomotives of a given type would form one unit, steel rails of a given weight another, station house of a given structure another, water-wheels of a certain pattern another, and so on.

Analyzing Cost of Industrial Plant

A plant generating electricity may be run by either steam or water power. The fixed charges on a steam plant being much greater than on a water power plant, the economy of the latter makes it desirable when conditions are such that its use is possible. Following the general classification of plant values given on page 15, the component parts of a hydroelectric plant may be subdivided as follows:[1]

TABLE 1—SUBDIVISION OF COST OF INDUSTRIAL PLANT

		Proportional Cost
I. Plant:		
(a) Riparian rights for dam and flowage basin, real estate expenses, organization expenses, preliminary legal expenses, cost of financing, removal of railroads, highways, bridges, and all expenses preliminary to actual construction of work.....		20%
(b) Permanent construction, dam, power house and waterways, etc....		30%
(c) Transmission system:		
(1) Right of way....	4.5	
(2) Copper	1.5	
(3) All else....	7.0	13%
II. Equipment:		
(a) Equipment of power house....		14%

[1] The data on hydroelectric plant used in this chapter are taken from the discussions of Calvert Townley and Dr. Cary T. Hutchinson, before the American Institute of Electrical Engineers, December 30, 1909.

III. Capitalized General Expenditures:

(a) General expense, engineering administration, legal, etc.	11%
(b) Interest during construction	12%

Of these items only I-b, I-c and II-a, comprising 57% of the entire cost of the plant, are subject to depreciation, and of item I-b a large part does not depreciate to any appreciable degree from physical causes, since it covers rock excavation and concrete.

Table 1 indicates the proportional cost of the main subdivisions of the plant. Thus the cost of the equipment is 14%, and of the transmission system 13%, of the total cost of the plant. Tables 2 and 3 indicate what percentage the cost of the different units of equipment and transmission system is of the total cost of the equipment and transmission system, respectively.

Analysis of Transmission System

For illustrative purposes our attention will be confined to items I-c and II-a, as they will serve to indicate the effects of both functional and physical depreciation. The following table classifies the units of the transmission system (I-c), indicating the proportional cost of the units and their lifetime in years. In this connection it may be well to repeat that by unit is meant one, or more than one, item of plant, as already explained.

Table 2—Cost and Lifetime of Transmission System

1. Transmission Line

		Proportional Cost	Life in Years
I-c-1	Right of way	45.0	..
I-c-2	Towers	18.4	15
I-c-3	Special structures	5.1	10
I-c-4	Insulators	2.1	10

I-c-5	Copper	23.7	25
I-c-6	Installation	5.7	..
		100.0	

2. Sub-Stations

		Proportional Cost	Life in Years
I-c-7	Land	6	..
I-c-8	Buildings	30	25
I-c-9	Transformers	40	20
I-c-10	Switches, etc.	16	10
I-c-11	Installation	8	..
		100	

Analysis of Power House Equipment

The equipment of power house is classified in the following table:

Table 3—Cost and Lifetime of Power House Equipment

		Proportional Cost	Life in Years
II-a-1	Stop logs, gates, and other wood exposed to air and water	0.80	5
II-a-2	Flooring, roofing, hardware, and miscellaneous fixtures	9.80	15
II-a-3	Tile wainscoting, sewage, plumbing system, metal window frames, etc.	2.45	15
II-a-4	Electric light and telephone	0.80	10
II-a-5	Switchboard equipment	4.35	10
II-a-6	Cables and heavy wiring	3.90	10
II-a-7	Cranes	1.25	15
II-a-8	Water-wheels	33.75	25
II-a-9	Water-wheel governors	2.90	10
II-a-10	Generators and transformers	40.00	25
		100.00	

Relation of Unit Cost to Investment

If the cost of the entire plant is known, the cost of

any unit can easily be derived by first finding what percentage the chief subdivision of which the unit forms a part, is of the cost of the plant, and taking this percentage of the entire cost of the plant. When the value of the chief subdivision is thus found, the value of the unit may then be determined by finding what percentage the unit is of the chief subdivision.

To illustrate, if the cost of the entire plant is $100,000, then the cost of the power house equipment is 14% of that amount, or $14,000, and the cost of any unit composing the power house may be found by multiplying $14,000 by the percentage of the cost of equipment represented by it. Thus the cost of the water-wheels is .3375 of $14,000, or $4,725. These percentages must, of course, be based upon the actual cost of the properties.

CHAPTER III

THE PLANT LEDGER

Character of Plant Ledger

The "plant ledger" should be made an essential part of the double-entry books, and be controlled by a Plant account in the general ledger with which it must be in agreement. The form and arrangement of the plant ledger should be such as to combine brevity, accuracy, and compactness with the necessary amount of detail. It should afford a complete record of the life of each unit or class of units of the plant. In determining what shall be considered a unit or class of units, an analysis of plant similar to that in the preceding chapter should be made.

The plant ledger must show not only the original investment in a unit of plant, but also in all additional units of a like character afterwards purchased. It must show as well the losses sustained each year on all wasting assets and their resultant diminished value. If desirable, the month may be made the time basis for figuring depreciation, but in most cases the yearly basis will be sufficiently accurate, and is employed in the following illustrations. The plant ledger should also be so arranged that all needed adjustments, either to show the effect of functional depreciation, or that of an unanticipated shortening or lengthening of a unit's life, can be made.

Description of Plant Ledger

A loose-leaf book is most suitable for the plant ledger, because it is unnecessary to carry in it more pages or sheets of paper than are needed for current work, and additions can be made when required. Forms 1 to 3 represent pages of the plant ledger. An explanation of the data entered in these forms is given below.

In the plant ledger the pages or sheets used for the record of any unit or class of units should be numbered consecutively to prevent confusion. The name of the unit appears in the upper left-hand corner. The year of installation of a new unit, or of adjustment of an old one, appears in the first column. In case of an old plant it indicates the year the plant ledger was installed. In the next column is entered the estimated life (or remaining life) of the unit, and in the third column its value at time of installation. In the remaining columns the annual depreciation allowances are distributed, their total equaling the cost or adjusted value of the unit, as given in column three, the element of scrap value not being taken into consideration.

The first distribution column of any particular unit should correspond in date with the year of installation of the property. Approximate accuracy will be secured if for the first year the distribution allowance be calculated as one-half that of a full year, since the installations will be fairly well scattered through it, some going into operation early, others late, in the year.

If a number of items of a class are installed at different times during the year, or if there may be uncertainty as to whether the installations for the year in any particular class are completed, an auxiliary blank should be used from which at the close of the year a recapitulation can be made and the total installation entered in the plant ledger. In this way one line serves for each year's installations of any class, and the work of computing the annual allowances and possible future adjustments is reduced to a minimum.

Use of Plant Ledger

To illustrate the working of the plant ledger, we may take the hydroelectric plant analyzed in the preceding chapter, assuming its total investment value to be $100,000, and selecting one of its units. For example, let us take item 9 of power house equipment, "Water-Wheel Governors," having an estimated life of ten years, and comprising 2.9% of the value of the equipment, or $406. Assuming the installation to have been made in the year 1910, the entry for it in the plant ledger is shown in Form 1. As, according to our assumption, but one-half of a full year's depreciation occurs in the year of installation, the distribution of the depreciation will extend over eleven columns in the ledger, a similar half-year's charge being made in the eleventh column, or for 1920.

If no additional installations are made; if functional depreciation does not diminish the value more rapidly than physical depreciation; and if our estimate of the unit's lifetime has been correct, or nearly correct, no adjustments will be required except the annual deduction of the depreciation allowance from the balance brought forward from the previous year. In such a case the record of this unit, when it has become worn out, appears in Form 1.

Adjustments may be required, however, at times during the lifetime of the unit for either of two reasons: First, obsolescence or inadequacy may so impair the functional value of the unit that its investment value drops below what the plant ledger indicates. Secondly, with the passage of time, it may be found that the lifetime of the unit was incorrectly estimated, necessitating the distribution of its remaining value on a new basis, as illustrated by the problem on page 45.

PLANT LEDGER Sheet No. ________

Unit Name or Number *Water-wheel Governors*

YEAR OF INSTALLATION OR ADJUSTMENT	ESTIMATE OF LIFE	ORIGINAL VALUE	ANNUAL DEPRECIATION BURDEN 1910	1911	1912	1913	1914	1915	1916	1917	1918	1919	1920	1921	1922	1923	1924
1910	10 years	$406.00	$20.30	40.60	40.60	40.60	40.60	40.60	40.60	40.60	40.60	40.60	20.30				
		Summary															
		$406.00															
Scrapped 1920		406.00															
		0.00															
Balance brought forward			$406.00	385.70	345.10	304.50	263.90	223.30	182.70	142.10	101.50	60.90	20.30				
Deduct Depreciation {a physical			20.30	40.60	40.60	40.60	40.60	40.60	40.60	40.60	40.60	40.60	20.30				
{b functional			0.00	0.00	0.00	0.00	0.00	0.00	0.00	0.00	0.00	0.00	0.00				
Total			$20.30	40.60	40.60	40.60	40.60	40.60	40.60	40.60	40.60	40.60	20.30				
Depreciated Balance		$406.00	$385.70	345.10	304.50	263.90	223.30	182.70	142.10	101.50	60.90	20.30	0.00				
Add cost of Installation of year following			0.00	0.00	0.00	0.00	0.00	0.00	0.00	0.00	0.00	0.00	0.00				
Balance forwarded		$406.00	$385.70	345.10	304.50	263.90	223.30	182.70	142.10	101.50	60.90	20.30	0.00				

Form 1. Plant Ledger (showing distribution of depreciation)

PLANT LEDGER — Sheet No. ______

Unit Name or Number *Water-wheel Govrnors*

YEAR OF INSTALLATION OR ADJUSTMENT	ESTIMATE OF LIFE	ORIGINAL VALUE	ANNUAL DEPRECIATION BURDEN														
			1910	1911	1912	1913	1914	1915	1916	1917	1918	1919	1920	1921	1922	1923	1924
1910	10 years	$406.00	$20.30	40.60	40.60	40.60	40.60	~~40.60~~	~~40.60~~	~~40.60~~	~~40.60~~	~~40.60~~	~~20.30~~				
								27.27	27.27	27.27	27.27	27.27	13.65				
Scrapped 1920		Summary $406.00 406.00 0.00															
Balance brought forward			$406.00	385.70	345.10	304.50	263.90	150.00	122.73	95.46	68.19	40.92	13.65				
Deduct Depreciation { a. physical			20.30	40.60	40.60	40.60	40.60	27.27	27.27	27.27	27.27	27.27	13.65				
b. functional			0.00	0.00	0.00	0.00	73.30	0.00	0.00	0.00	0.00	0.00	0.00				
Total			$20.30	40.60	40.60	40.60	113.90	27.27	27.27	27.27	27.27	27.27	13.65				
Depreciated Balance		$406.00	$385.70	345.10	304.50	263.90	150.00	122.73	95.46	68.19	40.92	13.65	0.00				
Add cost of Installation of year following		0.00	0.00	0.00	0.00	0.00	0.00	0.00	0.00	0.00	0.00	0.00	0.00				
Balance forwarded		$406.00	385.70	345.10	304.50	263.90	150.00	122.73	95.46	68.19	40.92	13.65	0.00				

Form 2. Plant Ledger (showing adjustment of value)

PLANT LEDGER

Unit Name or Number *Water-wheel Governors* Sheet No.____

YEAR OF INSTALLATION OR ADJUSTMENT	ESTIMATE OF LIFE	ORIGINAL VALUE	ANNUAL DEPRECIATION BURDEN 1910	1911	1912	1913	1914	1915	1916	1917	1918	1919	1920	1921	1922	1923	1924	1925	1926
1910	10 years	$406.00	$20.30	40.60	40.60	40.60	40.60	~~40.60~~	~~40.60~~	~~40.60~~	~~40.60~~	~~40.60~~	~~20.30~~						
								27.27	27.27	27.27	27.27	27.27	13.65						
1916	10 years	200.00							10.00	20.00	20.20	20.00	20.00	~~20.00~~	~~20.00~~	~~20.00~~	~~20.00~~	~~20.00~~	~~10.00~~
														27.50	27.50	27.50	27.50		
		Summary																	
		406.00																	
		200.00																	
		606.00																	
Scrapped 1920		406.00																	
		200.00																	
Scrapped 1924		200.00																	
		0.00																	
Balance brought forward			$406.00	385.70	345.10	304.50	263.90	150.00	322.73	285.46	238.19	190.92	143.65	110.00	82.50	55.00	27.50		
Deduct Depreciation a. physical			20.30	40.60	40.60	40.60	40.60	27.27	37.27	47.27	47.27	47.27	33.65	27.50	27.50	27.50	27.50		
Deduct Depreciation b. functional			0.00	0.00	0.00	0.00	73.30	0.00	0.00	0.00	0.00	0.00	0.00	0.00	0.00	0.00	0.00		
Total			$20.30	40.60	40.60	40.60	113.90	27.27	37.27	47.27	47.27	47.27	33.65	27.50	27.50	27.50	27.50		
Depreciated Balance		$406.00	$385.70	345.10	304.50	263.90	150.00	122.73	285.46	238.19	190.92	143.65	110.00	82.50	55.00	27.50	0.00		
Add cost of Installation of year following		0.00	0.00	0.00	0.00	0.00	0.00	200.00	0.00	0.00	0.00	0.00	0.00	0.00	0.00	0.00	0.00		
Balance forwarded		$406.00	$385.70	345.10	304.50	263.90	150.00	322.73	285.46	238.19	190.92	143.65	110.00	82.50	55.00	27.50	0.00		

Form 3. Plant Ledger (showing added installation and readjustment of value)

Adjustments for Obsolescence or Inadequacy

Let us assume that in the year 1914 certain causes lead to an abrupt fall in value, resulting from functional depreciation, the reduced value of the unit being found to be, according to principles stated on pages 29, 30, $150. The balance brought forward for the year, as shown in Form 2, is $263.90, and the physical depreciation for the year is $40.60, leaving $223.30, or $73.30 excess over actual value. This amount must therefore be deducted as functional depreciation. Owing to this extraordinary deduction, it will be necessary to make a new distribution over the remaining years of the plant's life on the basis of the remaining value, $150. A red line should be drawn through the future distributions on the basis of old value and a new distribution made on the next line below. These alterations are shown in Form 2. No new entry is made in the column headed "Original Value," except in case of purchase of additional property.

Adjustments for Physical Depreciation

If, after a number of years, experience shows that the original estimate of lifetime was in error, a somewhat similar adjustment should be made; not, however, by altering the amount remaining to be depreciated, but by extending it over a greater or less number of years, thus decreasing or increasing the remaining annual charges. Such an adjustment is shown in Form 3, for the item installed in the year 1916.

The correctness of the work of a sheet may be checked by finding the total of the future distributions, which should be equal to the last depreciated balance.

In case of a sudden heavy fall in values due to functional depreciation, its deduction in the revenues of the current year would create an excessive burden. It might then be well to spread the extra charge over a period of, say, two or three years, by dividing it into as many equal parts. Thus in Form 2 the functional depreciation, amounting to $73.30, would be divided into three parts of $24.43 each and deducted over the three-year period 1914, 1915, and 1916, an equal amount each year.

In this somewhat extraordinary instance there would be a difference of twice $24.43, or $48.86—the amount not deducted in the current year—between the depreciated balance and the extensions in the depreciation columns; for while the latter are based entirely on the reduced value of the property, the former has not been reduced by the full amount. But as soon as the full amount of the functional depreciation has been deducted, the two will again be equal.

How Plant Ledger is Controlled

As suggested, the plant ledger is controlled by the Plant account in the general ledger. Instead, however, of merely agreeing with its controlling account, as is usual with subordinate ledgers, the plant ledger should be in a twofold agreement with its controlling account; or perhaps it might be expressed by saying that it must agree with both the Plant account and the Depreciation Reserve account. For, whenever any accounts are charged in the plant ledger, the controlling Plant account is charged with an equal amount, the only difference being that the charges are subdivided in the plant ledger among the proper accounts; whereas their total is carried to the controlling account. Likewise, whenever any account is credited in detail in the plant ledger, which is done only when a unit of plant is scrapped, there will be an equal debit made to the Reserve for Depreciation account in the general ledger. It follows that while the first cost of all existing units of plant is shown in detail in the plant ledger and in total in the Plant account in the general ledger, the actual depreciated value is indicated by the difference between the Plant account and the Reserve for Depreciation, shown best in the balance sheet by deducting the latter from the former, as explained in Chapter IV.

Reserve Indicates Composite Depreciation

If no renewals or replacements whatever were made to the plant, the continually increasing reserve for depreciation would indicate the growth of composite depreciation, which would finally consume the entire value of the plant. But as soon as they are needed, renewals are made, and after a time they entirely counterbalance the effects of depreciation, with the result that the reserve for depreciation indicates the extent to which at any time the composite depreciation of the entire plant has progressed.

Relation of Reserve to Replacements

As has been suggested in Chapter I, the tendency of composite depreciation to reduce plant values below original investment values may be avoided by making additions to plant to the extent that composite depreciation is not covered by actual renewals, the additions being in reality replacement of values lost through depreciation. If the records are properly kept the extent of the composite depreciation of the original investment will be at all times indicated by the depreciation reserve, and this will in turn serve to indicate the amount which may be invested in additional plant when it is not needed in actual replacements. It must be remembered, however, that reserve for depreciation is not changed by such additions, being reduced only when old units are scrapped.

The book value of the plant, i.e., the figure representing first cost, will therefore tend to increase over the figure indicating investment to an amount equal to the normal accumulated reserve for depreciation, which latter will continue to increase only so long as annual depreciation exceeds annual cost of replacement. After depreciation and actual replacement cost become equal, the plant is normal, and the depreciation reserve will tend to gravitate about a figure representing the ordinary amount to which depreciation may be allowed to progress without sufficiently impairing the plant's efficiency to make it more profitable to increase the replacements.

It may be unnecessary to add that the annual depreciation charge is found by totaling the sums deducted for depreciation for the year in the plant ledger.

The Depreciation Fund

If an actual depreciation fund is created, as suggested in Chapter IV, it would in itself indicate the amount of money to be expended on replacements in order to keep plant values up to 100% of the original investment, and as a result would tend to disappear, remaining equal to the depreciation reserve only in case all replacements made are actual replacements of property scrapped, and have the same cost as the property so scrapped. The other valid use of the fund would be the amortization of a percentage of the capital, thus permanently reducing the investment.

CHAPTER IV

DEPRECIATION RESERVES VS. DEPRECIATION FUNDS

The subject of reserves and funds occasions much misunderstanding. An examination of present-day practice shows no unanimity of opinion upon the use of these two words. Not only are they employed loosely, but interchangeably. Some writers have shown their true meaning, but in practice little uniformity exists. A variety of conditions makes the employment of reserves beneficial; this also applies to funds. Bad debts, contingencies, accommodation paper, bonded indebtedness, depreciation, etc., admit of their useful application.

Purpose of Depreciation Charges

The manipulation of depreciation on the books is quite apart from the study of the principles that govern its amount and the method of determining it. Depreciation charges are adjustments made at the end of a period to remedy discrepancies between book accounts and the things whose values they indicate. Such discrepancies are sometimes in approximate proportion to time expired; but again they bear no relation to time. An instance of the former is depreciation of houses from weathering;[1] of the latter, destruction by wind or fire. Between such extremes are other forms of deterioration, the extent of which is more or less directly proportionate to time. The amount of the depreciation having been determined, the

[1] Amortization, as applied to bonds, is a perfect example of values varying with passage of time.

accounts must indicate it and make provision for future replacement costs.

The nature of the asset usually indicates the manner in which it will depreciate, and perhaps suggests the best method of determining its amount. But this has been touched upon in another chapter. Let us now consider how to indicate these changes on the books and to forestall their effects.

Twofold Object in View

Two different things should be done, viz.: (1) write down book values to actual values,[2] carrying the amount written off to the Profit and Loss account, and (2) provide funds to replace the assets when worn out. Failure to distinguish carefully between these two procedures leads to much confusion. It is an axiom that capital, and therefore assets, must not be impaired, or the prosperity and even the existence of an enterprise will thereby be endangered. Corporations have their existence by the sanction of the State, and the preservation of their capital is obligatory; otherwise it is voluntary. In any event deterioration of the value of ordinary assets is to be deplored. Preservation of assets is not accomplished by the omission of the depreciation charge. Apparent preservation may be accomplished for a certain length of time, but this is in appearance only and evil will inevitably result sooner or later.

As noted, funds for future replacements must be provided. These should come out of the legitimate income of the business. The depreciation reserve indicates the sum that will be necessary to make such replacements, prevents its distribution as profits, but does not set it apart and

[2] This, of course, may be done without crediting the asset account, by deduction of a "reserve" account from the asset account.

label it for that specific purpose. This is accomplished by the establishment of a depreciation fund, requiring an entry, or entries, entirely distinct from the depreciation charge.

Reserves and Funds Distinguished

While the depreciation reserve tends to preserve assets by reducing apparent net profits to actual net profits, and so avoids distribution of capital as profits, future replacements will have to be made out of the general funds of the treasury. But there is no guarantee, other than the general policy of the management, that these will be sufficient. On the other hand, a fund designated on the books for a definite object, though not inviolate, does possess at least a partial guarantee that it will be so employed. To illustrate, Corporation X, owning a factory building costing \$50,000 and having an estimated lifetime of thirty years, forms a depreciation reserve each year, crediting an account entitled "Reserve for Depreciation of Factory Building" and charging Profit and Loss. In the balance sheet of X this is shown either as a liability, thus:

BALANCE SHEET OF COMPANY X, AS AT......

Factory Building.........	\$50,000	Capital	\$100,000
Other Assets.............	53,000	Reserve for Depreciation of Factory Building....	1,000
		Dividends Payable.......	2,000
	\$103,000		\$103,000

or, preferably, as a deduction from the corresponding asset, as it appears in the first balance sheet on the following page.

BALANCE SHEET OF COMPANY X, AS AT......

Factory Building..$50,000			Capital	$100,000
Less Reserve for			Dividends Payable.......	2,000
Depreciation....	1,000	$49,000		
Other Assets...........		53,000		
		$102,000		$102,000

This prevents impingement upon capital, by limitation of distributable funds as profits. Had no charge to depreciation been made, the balance sheet would have been:

BALANCE SHEET OF COMPANY X, AS AT......

Factory Building.........	$50,000	Capital	$100,000
Other Assets.............	53,000	Dividends Payable........	3,000
	$103,000		$103,000

and after payment of dividends:

BALANCE SHEET OF COMPANY X, AS AT......

Factory Building.........	$50,000	Capital	$100,000
Other Assets.............	50,000		
	$100,000		$100,000

leaving assets overvalued by $1,000.

The retention of sufficient funds, by means of the depreciation reserve, is the essential step. If these are permitted to remain a part of the general funds of the business, they are naturally reinvested and give rise to no further consideration.

The problem of interest will not arise. But if we

determine to earmark such funds and set them apart, further consideration is necessary.

Sinking Funds

Sinking funds bear a sufficiently close analogy to depreciation funds to make their consideration here valuable to illustrate principles. Provision is made in trust deeds for the creation of sinking funds to liquidate bonded indebtedness, by requiring specified amounts to be paid into the hands of a trustee at designated intervals. These instalments are permitted to accumulate at compound interest to pay the obligations, the liquidation of which is the purpose of the fund.

Depreciation Funds

Funds created for the replacement of buildings, machinery, etc., are not, it is true, controlled by contract obligations; consequently the management retains full power over them. Otherwise they do not differ from sinking funds. The same formulas that are employed to compute payments to a sinking fund may be applied to depreciation funds. Interest may be handled differently in the two cases as a matter of policy. If securities of other corporations are purchased for the depreciation fund, it may be more convenient to mingle the revenue derived therefrom with the general income of the business, instead of adding it to the fund. The reason for this is that sinking fund trustees make a specialty of investments and can readily handle interest falling due, thus avoiding an excessive unproductive cash balance in the trust fund. Industrial corporations cannot look after matters of detail not a part of their own business. Therefore income from funds in their control can be employed more productively in the business, and will more than compensate for larger payments to the funds made necessary when interest is not added to it.

Formation of the Reserve

In later chapters the writer has discussed several formulas for finding the sums that must be set aside to accumulate in a given time to a given amount. For convenience, two of these formulas are reproduced here. If equal instalments are allowed to accumulate at compound interest, as in a sinking fund, then let x represent the amount of each instalment, v the amount to which the fund is to accumulate, r the rate of interest plus 1, and n the number of years to run; then,

$$(1) \qquad x = v \frac{(r-1)}{(r^n - 1)}$$

Logarithms may be employed to solve this formula if the term of years is large, say more than twelve, because of the difficulty of raising r to the nth power by multiplication. But if interest is not added to the principal, the amount of each instalment is determined thus:

$$(2) \qquad x = \frac{v}{n}$$

v being the sum accumulated after n years by paying equal instalments, x, into the fund.

Taking the simpler case first, if Corporation Y wishes to establish a replacement fund for, say, a building costing $25,000, with an estimated life of twenty-five years, by application of formula (2), we find the amount of each instalment to be $1,000, thus:

$$x = \frac{25{,}000}{25} = 1{,}000$$

Assuming that each year's depreciation amounts to $1,000, this is brought into the books by the following entry:

Profit and Loss..................................	$1,000.00	
To Reserve for Depreciation of Building....		$1,000.00

Formation of the Fund

Next, having decided to establish a depreciation fund for replacement of the building, and having found a suitable manner in which to invest the $1,000, the following entry is made:

Depreciation Fund for Building..................	$1,000.00	
To Cash..................................		$1,000.00
For investment in, etc.		

The balance sheet will then appear thus:

BALANCE SHEET OF COMPANY Y, AS AT......

Building................	$25,000	Capital.................	$50,000
Other Assets............	25,000	Reserve for Depreciation of Building...........	1,000
Depreciation Fund for Building.............	1,000		
	$51,000		$51,000

or, better still:

BALANCE SHEET OF COMPANY Y, AS AT......

Building................	$25,000	Capital.................	$50,000
Less Depreciation Reserve	1,000		
	$24,000		
Other Assets............	25,000		
Depreciation Fund for Building.............	1,000		
	$50,000		$50,000

If no depreciation fund is established, the balance sheet will be:

BALANCE SHEET OF COMPANY Y, AS AT......

Building	$25,000	Capital	$50,000
Less Reserve for Depreciation	1,000		
	$24,000		
Other Assets............	26,000		
	$50,000		$50,000

At the expiration of twenty-five years the depreciation reserve, having grown to the amount of the original building account, this account will vanish from the balance sheet, and the replacement will be made thus:

Cash	$25,000.00	
To Depreciation Fund for Building.......		$25,000.00
For sale of investment in, etc.		
Building	25,000.00	
To Cash................................		25,000.00
For construction of new building.		

Of course, in practice such simplicity is impossible, but the principles apply, subject to adjustments for residual values, variation from expected lifetime of assets, etc.

If the sinking fund method of adding interest to principal is followed, the computations are a little more complicated. Suppose Corporation Y possesses a machine costing $100,000, with an estimated lifetime of ten years. A replacement fund is to be established, to accumulate at compound interest, 4% being the assumed rate. Applying formula (1)—shown on page 54—each annual instalment may be found as follows:

$$x = \$100,000 \times \frac{1.04 - 1}{1.04^{10} - 1} = \$8,329.09$$

which is transferred to the depreciation fund by the same procedure as in the previous case. As interest is received on the investments in the depreciation fund, it is in turn invested in some suitable way, as follows:

Cash	\$......	
To Reserve for Depreciation		\$......
Depreciation Fund for Machine	....	
To Cash		....

Terminology

The terminology employed may be altered from that used in the foregoing explanation without changing the principle involved. Thus in railroad accounting the depreciation reserve is technically known as the "Reserve for Accrued Depreciation"; and in the balance sheet it is deducted from "Road and Equipment."

Advisability of Creating Funds

Of course it may not always be desirable to accumulate definitely tabulated sinking funds for replacements, and the presentation here is rather for the purpose of illustrating principles than of indicating the method to be pursued in any particular instance. The Interstate Commerce Commission definitely rejects this plan for purposes of railroad accounting, although it states that it is useful under other conditions. The character of the industrial plant must, to a large extent, determine the mode of financing renewals and replacements. There is good authority for the establishment of actual depreciation funds under proper conditions.[3] When making extensions

[3] See Proceedings, National Electric Light Association, June, 1909, Vol. 3, page 169.

to property, there would be no objection to borrowing money temporarily from the depreciation fund. But this borrowed money should be returned to the fund as soon as the money intended for the extension is secured through the sale of securities or otherwise.

A Study of Balance Sheets

A study of twenty-two balance sheets given in recent reports of large American corporations shows great lack of uniformity in the management of reserves and funds. A fair proportion of these concerns show reserves either as liabilities or as deductions from assets. Few indicate special funds, except sinking funds for the redemption of bonded indebtedness. The United States Steel Corporation balance sheet has an account on the asset side entitled "Sinking and Reserve Fund Assets." The Philadelphia Rapid Transit Company balance sheet shows "Reserve Fund for Renewals" on the asset side, and on the liability side, of equal amount, "Renewal Reserve." The balance sheet of the Third Avenue Railway Company has an account on the asset side entitled "Deposit for Depreciation, Renewals, and Contingencies," and on the liability side, "Reserve for Depreciation, Renewals, and Contingencies." The Pittsburgh Brewing Company has a "Plant Sinking Fund" among the assets.

Sinking funds receive equally diversified names. The International Paper Company has "Sinking Fund Accounts"; the United Gas Improvement Company, "Sinking Fund Securities"; the Interborough Rapid Transit Company, "Sinking Fund on 5%, 45-Year Gold Mortgage Bonds"; and the Bethlehem Steel Corporation, "Special Funds in Hands of Trustees for Redemption of Mortgages."

The following companies indicate the depreciation reserve on the right-hand side: Philadelphia Rapid Transit Company, Third Avenue Railway Company, Tennessee Copper Company, Interborough Rapid Transit Company, and Bethlehem Steel Corporation.

Sears, Roebuck & Co. and the Lehigh Valley Railroad Company show the reserve as a deduction from the assets. The report of Wells, Fargo & Co. as of June 30, 1912, indicates "Reserve for Accrued Depreciation" deducted from property and equipment account, whereas the report for the preceding year lists it on the liability side—an indication of progress.

The Utah Copper Company balance sheet shows an account on the liability side entitled "Appropriated Surplus—Sinking Fund"; while the balance sheets of Wm. Cramp & Sons, the Baldwin Locomotive Works, the International Harvester Company, the General Electric Company, the American Tobacco Company, and the Amalgamated Copper Company, indicate neither reserves nor funds of any kind.

These facts indicate a lack of uniformity, justifiable, perhaps, to a certain extent. Clearness in the balance sheet is, as a rule, aimed at; but in some cases it is difficult to believe that such is the intention. The balance sheet ought to reflect, not obscure, conditions. The proper tabulation therein of the depreciation reserves and funds is of much assistance to a clear and consistent presentation of facts.

CHAPTER V

DEPRECIATION AND EFFICIENCY

Relation of Depreciation to Efficiency

Every plant must be maintained at a certain degree of efficiency, to enable it to meet the various demands made upon it for service. In some cases, such as the telephone business, the general efficiency must be kept very high, otherwise dissatisfaction with the service soon appears. While a close connection exists between efficiency and depreciation, a distinction must at the same time be recognized. Of course, a loss of efficiency in a unit of plant must in time inevitably occur as the result of depreciation. But loss of efficiency of the whole plant does not occur in any degree proportionate to loss by depreciation. In fact, composite depreciation of plant may give rise to little or no loss of efficiency.

The failure to distinguish between depreciation and efficiency may account for the failure of many managements to make due allowance for depreciation. Oftentimes it is said that this or that machine is as good as new, after being used, say, ten or fifteen years; and as the time of discard seems indefinite, nothing is written off. It is true that the element of uncertainty is always present even in the most careful attempts to make depreciation allowances. But much of the confusion arises from a failure to recognize the essential difference between loss of efficiency and loss of capital assets through depreciation.

City of Beloit vs. Beloit Water, Gas and Electric Company

Buildings, machines, tools, etc., remain in unimpaired efficiency for years. But sooner or later they must wear out or become obsolete or inadequate. In this connection, the statement of the Wisconsin Railroad Commission in City of Beloit *v.* Beloit Water, Gas and Electric Company[1] is of interest, being to the effect that erroneous ideas of the value of property that has been in use for some time without requiring extensive repairs, are apt to be formed; but that the time always comes when a casual observation can detect the loss of value.

Efficiency Defined

Depreciation and efficiency must be carefully distinguished, the difficulty being due partly to a confusion or misunderstanding of the terms.

Efficiency is a word of frequent occurrence in modern business parlance. It applies both to labor and to machinery. As to machinery it raises questions of construction, adequacy, suitability, and general usefulness. It is the practical test of present effectiveness, to which most other considerations are subordinate. Beauty of architecture in buildings and gracefulness of construction in machines are desirable, but under competitive conditions such considerations give way to the all-important question of efficiency. Efficiency is prized and sought after; inefficiency is shunned and despised. In men, efficiency consists in highly specialized or broadly developed faculties; in machines, in powerful construction or delicately adapted mechanisms. Its possession is always coveted, and its loss always regretted.

The Factors of Value

But efficiency, the test of present usefulness, is not the only factor that determines value. Value depends upon present usefulness, it is true, but it also depends upon the

[1] 7 W. R. C. R. 187, 235, decided July 19, 1911.

length of time over which such usefulness will continue. Two similar machines may be equally efficient today; but one may continue to be useful for two years and the other for four. Can we say that they have equal value? There may be some uncertainty in individual cases; but the uncertainty is limited within certain bounds, and to a great degree vanishes when averages are considered, just as the uncertainties of lifetime vanish when large numbers of lives are considered. The lifetime of a single freight car is very uncertain, but the average lifetime of a thousand cars is ascertainable to the fraction of a year.

Depreciation—What It Is

The significance of the words depreciation and efficiency cannot be too clearly grasped. Depreciation is necessarily a somewhat theoretical and uncertain quantity. Broadly speaking, it includes wear and tear, obsolescence, and inadequacy. It may not be possible to give an all-inclusive definition of depreciation; rather its significance in each concrete case ought to be carefully studied. The Interstate Commerce Commission, the New York Public Service Commission, and similar bodies do not say just what and how much must be included in the depreciation charge, but leave this largely to the individual corporations to determine.

Individual peculiarities and customs will have their weight in determining the depreciation charge. Thus, if repairs are adequately met out of revenue, the annual provision for depreciation may be materially smaller than if they are neglected, owing to the greater longevity of property adequately repaired.

Comparison of Depreciation and Efficiency

Form 4 represents the character of depreciation figured on a straight line basis, also of efficiency, both curves applying to the same unit of plant. If the distance from *o* to *x* represents the efficiency of a new machine, or 100%, and the distance from *o* to *y* represents the lifetime of the same machine, say, ten years, then the straight line *xy* represents the progress of the theoretical straight line depreciation, while the curved line *xcy* indicates the rapidity with which efficiency declines.

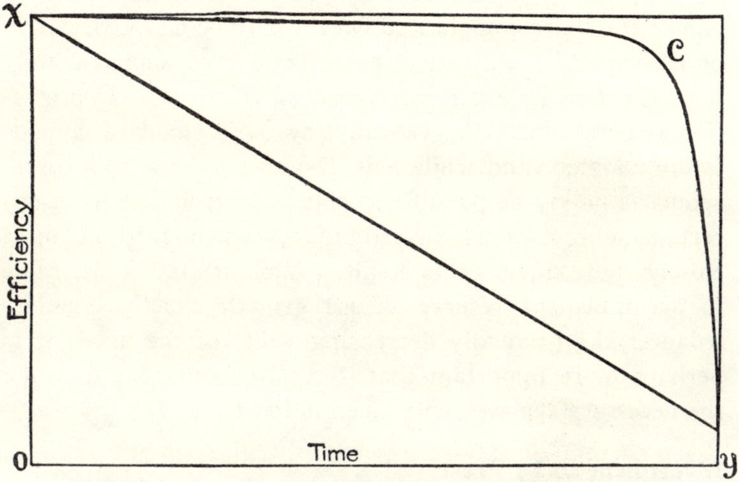

Form 4. Curves Showing Progress of Uniform Depreciation and of Diminishing Efficiency

From this diagram it will be seen that, whereas the efficiency of the machine continues almost unimpaired until the tenth year, the theoretical straight line depreciation reduces the value of the machine by an equal amount, nearly 10%, each year. Objection may be made on the ground that this straight line does not represent actual depreciation, and that should a sale occur at the end of the fifth or sixth year the machine would very likely bring considerably more or less than 50% of cost. Although this is true, it should be remembered that depreciation is usually figured with reference to future replacement, not future sale.

From this standpoint it does not ordinarily matter greatly if theoretical and actual depreciation do differ considerably at times during the life of a unit. Actual depreciation is always somewhat indeterminate, yet it is a consideration of vital importance in valuation work.

In place of the straight line to represent depreciation, one of the more complicated curves may be adopted, but in no case would such a curve correspond even approximately with the line indicating decrease of efficiency. Depreciation is determined, theoretically, by the method of computation adopted; and while it is desirable to have this correspond as nearly as possible to actual depreciation, it is uncertain, except after investigation, which method most closely approximates this result. While it may be desirable to accumulate a reserve whose growth exactly counterbalances the gradually decreasing value of the asset, it is perhaps more important that it shall be sufficient to make the necessary replacements when desired.

Investment to be Preserved

From what has been said it is apparent that while in the long run efficiency is dependent upon the extent to which depreciation has occurred, it may for a long time remain quite independent of accruing depreciation. High present efficiency ought not, therefore, to be used as an excuse for failing to make adequate provision for depreciation. Such a short-sighted policy can only lead to difficulties later on. Not merely efficiency must be retained, but the investment as well, and for the continued prosperity of the concern one is as necessary as the other.

Efficiency is the test of present daily effectiveness. Depreciation is the slow process by which industrial plant, whatever its present effectiveness may be, gradually approaches the time of discard and replacement.

Efficiency Not to be Impaired

In case of extensive plants, as water works, electric railways, and so on, a composite condition results from the existence of a large number of units of plant of different kinds in various stages of depreciation. Constant repairs and replacements prevent the plant as a whole from dropping in value below a certain percentage of cost new, or cost of reproduction. If we assume that normal depreciated plant value is 80% of reproduction cost, it is evident that the original investment has depreciated 20% in spite of renewals. But efficiency should remain at 100% as long as all necessary repairs and replacements are made; and the producing power of the plant should be increased if, instead of amortizing capital, replacement of values lost through composite depreciation is made by the purchase of additional plant.

There are other reasons why an old plant should possess a larger earning power than a new one, such as adaptability and smoothness of operation. These are also additional reasons for distinguishing between efficiency and depreciation.

Part II—Practical Applications

CHAPTER VI

REGULATION BY COURTS AND COMMISSIONS

The State's Relation to Industry

It is in accord with our present theory of government for the State to undertake in an increasing degree the regulation of industries. This is for the prevention of evils and the guarantee of good service to the public. This tendency assumes many and varied forms as it develops and extends into new fields. It has arisen because of the failure of competition to secure good service and proper treatment for all. In some cases the transactions of corporations are regulated with extreme minuteness, from general principles of policy to the details of daily routine.

The Importance of Accounts

An essential feature of any extensive business undertaking is its system of accounts. It concerns both the proprietorship and the public, frequently determining a policy that may benefit or injure the one or the other. It is not surprising, therefore, that accounting systems, methods, and theories have become the subject of legislative and judicial attention. With the rapid growth of corporate enterprise and the readiness with which large numbers of persons become co-sharers in the capital stock of big concerns, however small their respective holdings, there arises the problem of safeguarding their interests. When, owing to absence, ignorance, or other cause, they have no voice in the management of the enterprise which they promote by their investments and to which they look for an increase in, or at least the preservation of, their wealth, they demand a certain amount of protection from the State.

The stockholder is chiefly interested in two things—the preservation of his capital, and the income derived from it. He reads his company's annual report, trusting that the facts are as indicated in the balance sheet and the profit and loss statement. If they are not, he has neither the assurance that his dividend is the real amount of his income nor that his capital is unimpaired. If all proper charges have been made against gross profits for the fiscal period, his dividends represent true profit. If not, profits are overstated and capital is decreased to the extent of the error.

Meaning of "Net Profits"

Practically all the states have enacted laws to the effect that dividends must be paid only from net profits; but there is some question as to the significance of the phrase "net profits," and a lengthy combat has resulted over the question of the inclusion of an annual depreciation charge among the more obvious expenses. Yet, of all expenses, this is perhaps the least avoidable, and net profits do not exist until proper allowance has been made for it.

There is little disagreement in framing a definition of net profits in general terms, but trouble arises when we try to discover the detailed deductions that must be made from gross profits to arrive at net profits. Thus an English court declares net profits to be the excess of current gains over the working expenses, as indicated by the revenue accounts;[1] and a New Jersey court says that net profit is the clear gain of a business venture shown after deducting the invested capital, the expenses of operation, and losses sustained.[2]

---

[1] *In re* London, etc., Bank, 72 L. T. 227; aff'd (1885), 2 Ch. 166.
[2] Park *v.* Grant Locomotive Works, 40 N. J. Eq. 144; 3 Atl. 162.

Division of opinion over these statements first occurs when we attempt to detail the actual working expenses, expenses of operation, and losses sustained.

The meaning of these definitions is that capital must not be impaired by declaring dividends out of it under the guise of profits. To say that capital must not be parceled out as dividends and that dividends must be declared out of net profits, is merely viewing the matter from different points. The former expression is used when capital has been deliberately encroached upon, as in Appleton *v.* American Malting Company,[3] where no question existed as to impairment of capital. The latter expression applies when the bulk of the dividend is proper but in addition to its inclusion of net profits it includes a little capital also.

Preservation of Capital

When capital is deliberately distributed through dividends, there is no ground for dispute. The courts are in such close accord as to its illegality and the personal responsibility of the directors for the amount of such illegal dividends authorized, that little need be said about it. But upon approaching the subject from the other side, to learn what reservations must be made in order to insure preservation of the capital, the courts fail to satisfy us with either a clear or a consistent analysis. They point out and punish the gross offense, but they do not show how the evil results which that offense produces may be avoided when those effects result incidentally through the overpayment of dividends and consequent injury to capital. Thus, in the case of Belfast & M. L. R. Co. *v.* City of Belfast,[4] the court asserted that before dividends could be declared, several kinds of charges must be met. "Therefore," runs the de-

[3] 54 Atl. Rep. 454 (N. J.).
[4] 1 Atl. Rep. 362; 77 Me. 445.

cision, "if there is a bonded, funded, permanent, or standing debt, the interest on it must be reckoned out of net earnings. If there is a floating debt which it is not wise or prudent to place in the form of a funded debt, or to postpone for later payment, that should also be paid. If the financial situation of the company is such as to render it expedient to commence or continue the scheme of a sinking fund for the extinguishment of the company's indebtedness some day or other, an annual contribution out of the net earnings for that purpose would be reasonable. These deductions made from the net earnings, the balance will be the profits of the company distributable among stockholders."

Shall we say that the corporation, after conforming to the court's ruling, stood in no danger of impairing its capital? Although this was an early case, yet not without precedent,[5] the improvement since made—excepting a few decisions and the work of the Interstate Commerce Commission and of certain state public service commissions—has been slight.

Decisions on Depreciation

In the earlier case (1878) of Union Pacific R. R. *v.* United States[6] the Supreme Court gave an admirable definition of net profits: "Theoretically, the expenses chargeable to earnings include the general expenses of keeping up the organization of the company, and all expenses incurred in operating the works and keeping them in good condition and repair." This case was a precedent for the Maine court in Belfast & M. L. R. Co. *v.* City of Belfast cited above, and, presumably, shaped that decision to a certain extent. But the weakness of the decision is its failure to define

[5] The court quoted from the following in substantiation: Taft *v.* Railroad Co., 8 R. I. 316; St. John *v.* Erie Ry. Co., 10 Batchf. 271; S. C., 22 Wall. 136; Union Pacific R. R. *v.* U. S., 99 U. S. 402.

[6] 99 U. S. 402.

accurately what expenses are necessary to keep a railroad in good condition. Did the court mean to include therein all charges now indicated under the three heads, repairs, renewals and replacements, or did it refer to ordinary repairs only? The same decision is marred by the assertion that it is often better to charge betterments to revenue than to capital, which in itself is sufficient to upset all calculations as to net profits.

Depreciation a Proper Charge

In the same year that the decision in Union Pacific R. R. *v.* United States was given (1898), the Supreme Court in United States *v.* Kansas Pacific Railway Company[7] indicated that it limited the charges to gross profits to the expenditures actually incurred, refusing to accept as a proper charge to profits a sum indicated as necessary to put the road in proper repair but not actually expended. This case draws a clean line between current repairs on the one hand, and deferred renewals and replacements on the other. It is difficult to understand how, under this ruling, a reserve could be established for replacement, or how any plan of extending the cost of extensive repairs over a series of years could be pursued. In the light of recent decisions of the Interstate Commerce Commission it is easy to see the inconsistency in the definition of net profits given by the Supreme Court and in its attempt to apply it. In more recent decisions of the Supreme Court, notably City of Knoxville *v.* Water Company[8] and Willcox *v.* Consolidated Gas Company,[9] depreciation is regarded as a proper charge. In the former case the Supreme Court says that a company "is not bound to see its property gradually waste, without making provisions out of earnings for replacement," and

[7] 99 U. S. 459.
[8] 212 U. S. 1.
[9] 212 U. S. 19.

adds that it is privileged to keep its property unimpaired by the expenditure of earnings, in order that after a period of years the original value may be still maintained.

Our courts have done little to compel a regular charge to depreciation. Less conspicuous but more effective have been the efforts of public accountants—both in this country and in England—and also of bankers, to secure adequate depreciation charges. Many corporations now make regular depreciation charges in order to secure an unqualified audit certificate. Much time has been spent in clearing away false conceptions, and we are entering upon a period in which what at first appeared to be an improper charge, and then a legitimate one, is now regarded as a necessary one. The movement has been considerably aided by the publications of the Interstate Commerce Commission, which present the results of long experience on the part of railway accounting officers and public accountants. The method of charging depreciation employed by the Commission is the outcome of its attempt to aid itself and others in arriving at the facts in railroad administration.

How Depreciation Charge is Regulated

It is unusual for the commissions, in their prescription of uniform systems of accounting, to more than suggest the amount or even the method of determining the amount of the depreciation allowance. It is deemed best to leave this to the judgment of those most thoroughly acquainted with the conditions in each instance. Rather it is the principle of the accounting procedure that is enforced, since this allows room for variations in extent, rapidity, or character of depreciation. A brief description of the requirements of two leading commissions possessing plenary powers over public service companies, viz., the Interstate Commerce Commission and the New York

Public Service Commission for the First District, in so far as they refer to depreciation, will serve to show the present tendency.

Regulations of Interstate Commerce Commission

According to Act of Congress, the Interstate Commerce Commission is given power to prescribe uniform accounts for gas and electric corporations in the District of Columbia.[10] According to its published classification,[11] the accounts are divided into three fundamental classes: (1) operating revenue and expense accounts, (2) income accounts, and (3) balance sheet and capital accounts. Under these come the subdivisions, or primary accounts. Thus, for gas corporations, operating revenue falls into six distinct accounts, which are designated by symbolic letters with annexed numerals, as G101, G102, and so on. Operating expenses for gas corporations are divided into five general classes: (1) production expenses, (2) transmission and distribution expenses, (3) street and park lighting expenses, (4) commercial expenses, and, lastly, (5) general and miscellaneous expenses. Production expenses are separated into seventeen classes, four of which are maintenance accounts for work and station structures, power plant equipment, gas apparatus, and work tools, respectively. Transmission and distribution expenses are separated into nine classes, four of which are maintenance accounts for gas mains and services, gas meters, distribution tools, and gas appliances, respectively. Street and park lighting expenses are separated into two classes, one of which is a maintenance account for street lamps. General miscellaneous expenses are separated into sixteen classes, one of which is a maintenance account for general

[10] Effective January 1, 1910.

[11] Uniform System of Accounts for Gas Corporations and Electric Corporations in the District of Columbia.

structure, and a second is an account for general amortization. A similar classification is followed for electric corporations. It is in these maintenance accounts that the depreciation of the different capital accounts is expressed. In this connection it should be noted that the maintenance accounts and capital accounts are complements of each other.

Income accounts form the next general division. There are seventeen classes of these, the account for operating expenses being the one in which the depreciation costs or expenses as expressed in the maintenance and depreciation accounts are collected for deduction from gross income.

The third general division is composed of the balance sheet accounts. These indicate assets, liabilities, and capital. The asset accounts are twenty-five in number, and the liability and capital accounts fourteen in number. Liability account 37 is entitled "Accrued Amortization of Capital," and is complementary to operating expense account G174, entitled "General Amortization." To General Amortization (G174) an amount is charged monthly necessary to cover wear and tear, obsolescence, and inadequacy accrued during the month in the tangible capital, a reasonable amount for depreciation of intangible capital, and a sufficient amount to cover ordinary casualties, less the amounts charged for repairs in the various maintenance accounts. The amount so charged is in turn credited to liability account 37, "Accrued Amortization of Capital"; thus:

General Amortization (G174)....................	$.	
To Accrued Amortization of Capital.........		$.......
To cover depreciation, inadequacy, wear and tear, loss of intangible values, and extraordinary casualties, not covered in current maintenance for the month ending..........		

Purpose of the Reserve

It must be remembered that the reserve for accrued amortization of capital is what its name implies—an account to adjust depreciation not made good through maintenance. The need of such provision was indicated in Chapter I, "Character of Industrial Plant," since, particularly during the first ten or fifteen years of the utility's life, depreciation greatly exceeds maintenance costs. The Interstate Commerce Commission suggests that the corporation's experience during the preceding five years be considered in estimating depreciation. Permission is given to base the rate on the amount of gas sold. Whenever any capital is retired from service, the original money cost, less salvage, is charged to Accrued Amortization of Capital. This is proper, since the reserve has been accumulated to offset the depreciation, which amounts to cost less salvage. In case of property purchased before December 31, 1909, however, the depreciation applicable to the period following that date only, can be charged to Accrued Amortization of Capital. The depreciation accruing before that date should be charged to Profit and Loss, unless it was actually covered by a depreciation reserve. In the latter case it would be charged to such reserve account.

The plan adopted by the New York Public Service Commission, First District, differs only in detail from the above.[12]

Railroad Companies

Railroad companies doing interstate business maintain the following general accounts for operating expenses:[13]

---

[12] Uniform System of Accounts of Street and Electric Railways, effective January 1, 1909. Also Uniform System of Accounts for Electrical Corporations, effective January 1, 1909.

[13] Classification of Operating Expenses, third revised issue (I. C. C.).

1. Maintenance of Way and Structures
2. Maintenance of Equipment
3. Traffic Expenses
4. Transportation Expenses
5. General Expenses

Under these general accounts are grouped primary accounts. Included under the general account "Maintenance of Equipment," for instance, are twenty-nine primary operating expense accounts. Each subdivision of equipment—steam locomotives, passenger-train cars, electric equipment of cars, etc.—is given three separate primary operating expense, or maintenance, accounts for (1) repairs, (2) renewals, and (3) depreciation.

Classification of Depreciation Charges

The third revised issue of the classification of operating expense details the charges to be made to these accounts. Thus, to "Steam Locomotives—Repairs" are charged cost of material used, less salvage, and cost of labor in repairing steam locomotives and tenders and their fixtures. To "Steam Locomotives—Renewals" are charged original cost, record value, or purchase price of steam locomotives condemned, destroyed, or sold, less the amount previously charged to depreciation to date of retirement and the scrap value. For "Steam Locomotives—Depreciation" a monthly charge of a certain per cent of the original cost, record value, or purchase price, is made for the establishment of a reserve for future replacements. Steam locomotives are one of the seven classes of equipment upon which formal repair renewal and depreciation charges are required. These are:

1. Work equipment
2. Steam locomotives

3. Electric locomotives
4. Passenger-train cars
5. Freight-train cars
6. Electric equipment of cars
7. Floating equipment

Before the third revision of operating expenses became effective on July 1, 1907, repairs, renewals, and depreciation had been grouped in one account, "Repairs and Renewals." The change was made in the interests of better accounting, but in some quarters the impression gained ground that operating expenses would thereby be increased. This, as the Commission explained, would be the case only where property has not been maintained in the past. The amount charged for depreciation of property, as indicated, is credited to "Reserve for Accrued Depreciation." This is a balance sheet account and should be deducted from the investment account "Road and Equipment" for the purpose of showing actual work as at the date of the balance sheet. The Reserve for Accrued Depreciation is both an adjustment and a clearing account. It is a clearing account because when equipment is retired its cost, less salvage, is charged to this account.[14]

This appears to be an abandonment of the theory that railroads, owing to their extensive and varied assets, can with safety permit all charges for repairs, renewals, and replacements to be made to current revenue for the year or period in which repairs, renewals, and replacements are made. As a matter of fact depreciation to a certain extent, say, 15 or 20%, will occur no matter how varied or extensive the equipment. Such loss in the investment can be guarded against only through depreciation reserves. It is to be noted, however, that there is a differ-

[14] Accounting Series, Circular No. 120, case 567.

ence in the manner of handling such reservations under the plan suggested by the Interstate Commerce Commission, from that sometimes followed.

Two methods of handling depreciation reserves are in vogue—the insurance method and the sinking fund method. Under the sinking fund method a certain percentage of the value of a property is written off each year and accumulated by compound interest, the investments usually being made in outside securities, so that when the time for replacement arrives the fund will be sufficient to purchase the property necessary to make the replacement. This it will do if the cost of the replacement is the same as the original value of the property replaced, or, if greater in value, with an additional expenditure, which will be, not a replacement, but a betterment.

Under the insurance method, which is approved by the Interstate Commerce Commission, compound interest is not used, and the fund is not designated for the replacement of any specific part of capital; nor is the fund accumulated through the depreciation charge reserved until it can be expended in replacing the identical property upon which it was figured. Rather it is spent wholly or partly during the same year in which it is charged, by replacing other equipment or purchasing additional equipment. Of course, the entire accumulation need not be spent during the year in which it is accumulated. Business policy must determine whether replacements or new equipment shall be purchased, the decision lying with the board of directors.

Industrial Establishments

Whether desirable or not, such detailed supervision of depreciation is not always found in industrial establishments. Yet the interesting facts about a railroad company do not differ essentially from those which we wish to know concerning an industrial concern. We study both from similar documents—the balance sheet and the statement of profit and loss—and therein the vital points are similar. Although the assets are different in form, it is equally important that they be protected; and although the sources of income differ, the percentage of net profits measures the relative success of the undertakings.

Present and Future Conditions

The Interstate Commerce Commission has made clear that a charge may be made for repairs or renewals even though it be not all expended within the period covered by the statement of profit and loss. The Commission states that it is not intended to say that the entire accumulation of a year must be expended during the year.[15] This simplifies matters greatly. It makes it possible to write off a developmental expense over a series of years; also to accumulate a fund for the future replacements of expensive material assets.

The first steps having been taken in the direction of a compulsory depreciation charge, it remains to be seen how far the reform will extend. The State Utility Commissions are seconding the Interstate Commerce Commission by introducing in their work the principles of depreciation.

The chief factors that will make for or against a compulsory depreciation charge in the future are:

1. The general theory of the State's relation to industry.
2. The efficiency of corporate management when not interfered with by the State.

[15] Accounting Series, Circular No. 13, page 2.

3. The tendency of industries to organize in a way to invite control by commission.
4. The attitude of professional accountants and the candor with which they urge that which the State may compel if they fail.

CHAPTER VII

THE INCOME TAX

The Income Tax in England

In England taxation of incomes has served as a means of raising revenue longer than in the United States. Before 1878, English corporations, in the determination of their taxable incomes, were not allowed to make any deduction from income to cover depreciation. The law granted the deduction of actual expenditures for repairs and renewals, but not in excess of the average expenditures for the preceding three years. Allowance could not be made for existing depreciation unless money had been paid out to cover it. In 1878 the law was altered to permit the deduction of a reasonable amount for the diminished value of machinery and plant resulting from wear and tear. Depreciation was not mentioned in the law, nor was an allowance for obsolescence permissible. Buildings were not specifically mentioned in the Act.

In 1897 a complaint made to the Chancellor of the Exchequer brought the reply that no objection would be made to a deduction from the assessable profits of the year of so much of the replacement cost as was represented by the existing value of the replaced machinery. This allows nothing for composite depreciation. The Finance Act of 1907 provides that no allowance can be made in excess of an amount which, when added to previous allowances, equals in amount the cost of the plant plus any additional capital expenditures. The Finance Act of 1910 grants some further relief in the way of allowances for maintenance and repair of land and farm buildings.

English Income Tax Decisions

In the English case of Knowles *v.* McAdam (1877) a deduction from the income of a mine property to cover exhaustion of capital was permitted, but this decision was probably reversed in the case of Coltness Iron Company *v.* Black (1881), where the charging of the cost of sinking new shafts to replace old ones was not allowed. It seems, however, that there is no objection to an allowance for the cost of sinking a shaft when minerals are secured therefrom which are a source of profit for the year in which such shaft is sunk. In Coltness Iron Company *v.* Black the deduction disallowed did not represent the cost of shaft sinking during the year, but rather expenditure on borings and shafts exhausted during the year. The latter is the better basis, so the situation appears unsatisfactory.

The Income Tax in the United States

The first income tax law in the United States was enacted in 1861 and repealed in 1872. A tax of 2% on incomes in excess of $4,000 was levied by act of Congress in 1894, but this law was declared unconstitutional. In 1909 the so-called Corporation Tax Law was passed. Although nominally an excise tax, in many ways it resembled an income tax limited to corporations.

The Corporation Tax of 1909—Depreciation Charges

This act levied a tax of 1% upon the net income of corporations, joint-stock companies, or insurance companies, in excess of $5,000. In arriving at the net income of such concerns, deductions were allowed for expenses, interest, taxes, depreciation, and certain other items.

In returns to the Commissioner of Internal Revenue, the amounts allowed for depreciation were required to be stated separately from other losses. Detailed regulations were promulgated by the Treasury Department.[1] These provided that before depreciation could be allowed it must have actually occurred, and should be estimated with the aid of the best data obtainable from other similar properties. The depreciation was also charged off on the books of the corporation claiming it. It was not necessary, however, that the book value of the asset be itself reduced, for by a special ruling (May 9, 1912) permission was given to make such charges in the form of a nominal reserve, deductible from the corresponding asset.

The Treasury Department ruled that the deduction for depreciation should be based on four considerations: (1) the lifetime of the property, (2) its cost, (3) its value, and (4) its use; all evidenced by ledger entry as already noted. It is worthy of mention that in the regulations for the income tax of 1913, value is omitted from consideration, evidently with good reason.

The Corporation Tax of 1909—Stocks, Bonds, and Real Estate

Stocks and bonds owned could be adjusted annually, such adjustment being made a matter of ledger entry, and depreciation or appreciation deducted or added, as the case might be. Or, if held as permanent investments, no account could be taken of them until disposed of, when loss or gain over original investment was to be prorated and the amount belonging to the period since the incidence of the tax added to or deducted from gross income, as the case might be. Increase or decrease in the value of real estate sold, when not determinable for each year, could be similarly prorated. Allowance was not granted for premiums on stocks and bonds arbitrarily charged off. The shrinkage must have been actual. If buildings were voluntarily removed, as in

[1] Treasury Decisions 1727, 1742, 1754, and 1796.

case of replacement, the resulting loss, if not covered by depreciation already provided, was not allowed, but was considered as entering into the cost of the new structure. An allowance for depreciation of the corporation's own stock was not granted, as such a loss was not that of the corporation but of the stockholders. Identical treatment of stocks and bonds is not altogether proper, nor is the suggested method of bond valuation accurate.[2]

The Income Tax of 1913

The Excise Tax of 1909 has been superseded by the Income Tax of 1913. An amendment to the Constitution has removed the fundamental objection to this kind of tax, and it is now considered a fixed part of our fiscal system. Section 2 of the Act of Congress, October 3, 1913, provides, *inter alia*, that the net income of corporations and joint-stock companies shall be ascertained by deducting from the gross income received from all sources during the fiscal year: first, all ordinary and necessary expenses paid during the year in maintenance and operation, including rentals of property; second, all losses actually sustained during the year not compensated by insurance or otherwise, including a reasonable allowance for depreciation arising from use and wear and tear of property. In the case of mining corporations, the law also grants a reasonable allowance for the depletion of ores and all other material deposits, not in excess of 5% of the gross value, at the mine, of the output for the year for which the computation is made.

In the case of corporations existing under the laws of foreign countries, net income is ascertained by deducting the allowances, including depreciation, from the gross income accruing within the year from investments made and business transacted in the United States.

[2] See Sprague's "Accountancy of Investment."

For the determination of the income of individuals, the wording of the law, with respect to the allowance for depreciation, is slightly different than for corporations. For these latter a reasonable allowance is granted for depreciation resulting from use and wear and tear of property; for individuals a reasonable allowance is granted for depreciation resulting from exhaustion and wear and tear of property arising out of its employment in business. The difference is immaterial, however, and is not recognized in the regulations promulgated by the Commissioner of Internal Revenue.

Allowance for Exhaustion

The allowance for exhaustion and wear is for such as has occurred for the year assessed, not for preceding years.[3] In Addie & Sons *v.* Solicitor of Inland Revenue,[4] it was held that no deduction could be made for pit sinking or for depreciation of buildings and machinery. In Little Miami, etc., R. R. *v.* U. S.,[5] it was held that estimated depreciation of assets may be deducted. Sums carried to the surplus or contingent fund cannot be deducted, though afterwards lost.[6] Sums carried to account of a repair fund come within the above, and cannot be deducted.[7] In England depreciation of machinery due to removal of business is a capital loss and not deductible.[8] In Burnley Steamship Co. *v.* Aikin,[9] a steamship company was allowed a deduction on (1) loss of earning power from obsolescence, and (2) loss of market value from wear and tear. The Knoxville Water case and the Consolidated Gas case are com-

[3] Clayton *v.* Newcastle-under-Lyme, 2 Tax Cas. 416 (1888); Hall & Co. *v.* Rickman, 54 Week. Rep. 380 (1906).

[4] 1 Tax Cas. 1 (1875).

[5] 108 U. S. 277; 27 L. Ed. 724 (1883).

[6] Solicitor General Phillips, 14 Ops. Atty. Gen. 643 (1874).

[7] Ruling, 2 Int. Rev. Rec. 100.

[8] Smith *v.* Westinghouse Brake Co., 2 Tax Cas. 357.

[9] 3 Tax Cas. 275 (1894).

mented on elsewhere. Most of the cases are English, and so may not be a precedent for American courts.

In Great Britain the owner of both the mine and the estate of which the mine formed a part was not allowed a deduction for partial exhaustion of the mine.[10] The House of Lords, in Coltness Iron Co. *v.* Black,[11] held that a mine owner is not entitled to a deduction for capital expended in making bores and sinking pits which had been exhausted by the year's working, thus apparently overruling Knowles *v.* McAdam.[12] In Bonner *v.* Bassett Mines, Ltd.,[13] it was held that it was wrong to allow a deduction for a tin mine shaft sunk fifty fathoms further down for the purpose of discovering lodes. The money required for sinking the shaft was held to be a capital expenditure.

Stratton's Independence, Ltd., v. Howbert

This decision[14] is of considerable importance in determining the status of mining corporations under the income tax law and deserves special attention. Stratton's Independence, Ltd., was an English corporation engaged in mining in Colorado. Suit was brought in the District Court of the United States, District of Colorado,[15] by the corporation to recover taxes paid under protest to the Government for 1909 and 1910, under the Corporation Tax Act of 1909, on what was presumably income but which the corporation declared represented depreciation of its capital assets. Briefly, the point at issue was, what deductions should the corporation be permitted to make from gross income in order to arrive at taxable net income? No question was raised as to the appropriateness of deducting

[10] Miller *v.* Fairie, 16 Scot. L. R. 189 (1878).
[11] 1 Tax Cas. 287 (1881).
[12] 26 Week. Rep. 114 (1877).
[13] Law Times, Dec. 31, 1912, page 179.
[14] L. Ed. Advance Opinions, Jan. 15, 1914.
[15] No. 5781.

ordinary expenses of operation. Disagreement arose over the amount that should be allowed for depreciation of capital resulting from the extraction of ores.

It is agreed that income for purposes of dividends, in case of mining companies, may include a portion of the capital.[16] Therefore, the District Court held that if the net income for dividend purposes is not affected by the amount of the ores extracted, it should not be affected for purposes of the excise tax. From this and other statements made by the court in this case the inference might be drawn that no allowance whatever could be made for depletion of minerals. Thus the court suggests that the practical result of deducting depreciation of ores would be to free the company from payment of any tax whatever. In this instance such would be the case, because the company held that the depletion of the ores amounted to their actual selling price after being mined, less cost of extraction. This leaves no income whatever. It seems clear that the court's statement that depreciation as applied to buildings, etc., cannot be enlarged to apply to ore extracted, is made in view of the particular claims of the company.

The trial was based on an agreed statement of facts, to wit: that for the year 1909 the gross sales of ores amounted to $284,682.85; the cost of extracting the same, $190,939.42; and that the value of the ores thus extracted in 1909 was $93,743.43 when still in the mine. In other words, the difference between gross sales and cost of extraction exactly equaled the value of the ores before extraction. The facts for the year 1910 were similar.

The company appealed the case and on a certificate from the Circuit Court of Appeals the Supreme Court of the United States affirmed the decision of the lower court. Being made upon an agreed statement of fact, this decision

[16] See Morawetz on Private Corporations, § 442.

is in no way opposed to the Treasury decision permitting a reasonable deduction for the depreciation of ores on the basis of their value *in toto,* or on the basis of original cost as required under the Income Tax of 1913. The Supreme Court in its decision states that a definition of value of ore in place was adopted with the intention of excluding any allowance for profit, that it is fallacious to assume that the ores possessed any such value before they were mined, and that property is to be valued not on latent or occult values, but on practical considerations affecting market value.

No depreciation was charged on the mine's books, but the court did not express an opinion as to whether this was a matter of material importance.

Interpretation of the Income Tax Law

Under the Income Tax of 1913, the Commissioner of Internal Revenue prescribes that, in accordance with the law, the allowance for depreciation from exhaustion and wear and tear cannot, in the case of mines, exceed 5% of the gross value at the mine of the year's output. This does not include the expense of restoring property, nor can it include an allowance to make good exhaustion already allowed. By gross value at the mine is meant the actual market value of the output, coal, crude oil, etc., at the mine or well if the price is established by sale at that place. If established at some other place, or on the basis of bullion or metallic value, then such established value less transportation, reduction, and smelting charges is held to represent gross value at the mine.[17] The depreciation allowance must be based upon the shrinkage of the actual investment, and in case it appears that the established allowance may return the capital invested before the mine is exhausted, the allowance must be diminished in accordance with the estimated

[17] Income Tax Regulations, Acts 6 and 142.

number of years the minerals will last. If the capital invested is thus returned to the corporation before the minerals are exhausted, no further deduction shall be made.

How Deduction is Limited

A variation exists in the wording of the law in its application to mines owned by individuals and those owned by corporations.[18] In the former case it provides a reasonable allowance for exhaustion and wear and tear of property arising out of its use or employment in the business, not to exceed 5% of the gross value of the output in case of mines. But for corporations it says all losses sustained, including a reasonable allowance for depreciation by use and wear and tear of property; and in case of mines a reasonable allowance for depletion of ores and all other natural deposits, not to exceed 5% of the gross value of the output. The former would seem to limit the total deduction for depreciation to 5% of the gross value of the output at the mine; while the latter specifically states that a reasonable allowance shall be deducted for depreciation from use and wear and tear, if any, and an allowance for depletion of minerals, not in excess of 5% of the gross value of the output at the mine. Article 142 of the Income Tax Regulations indicates that in the interpretation of the law no such distinction should be made. In referring to the allowance for both individuals and corporations it says that if such rate of 5% will tend to return the investment before the deposits are exhausted, it should be reduced. Article 143 of the regulations specifically grants to corporations an allowance for depreciation of plant over and above the 5% for depletion of ores. There is no reason why individuals should be given less.

Following are comments on the regulations supplied by

[18] Income Tax Regulations, Acts 6 and 142.

the Commissioner of Internal Revenue. Likenesses and differences in the administration of the Income Tax of 1913 and the Corporation Tax of 1909 are noted.

Sale of Capital Assets

In case of property acquired after January 1, 1909, and later disposed of, the difference between cost and selling price shall constitute an addition to or subtraction from gross income of the year in which the property is sold, according as it represents a loss or a gain. In case of property acquired before January 1, 1909, such difference between cost and selling price should be prorated, and the amount of the difference applicable to the period since January 1, 1909, added to or deducted from gross income of the year in which the sale is made, accordingly as it is a gain or a loss.[19] This is the same provision as in the law of 1909.

Good-Will

No allowance is granted for depreciation of good-will.[20] This is the same as under the law of 1909.

Bad Debts

To be a proper deduction they must be charged off on the books, and treated as income if later collected.[21] This is the same as under law of 1909.

Reserve for Anticipated Losses

Not a proper deduction.[22]

Removal of Buildings

If not already charged to depreciation the loss thus in-

---

[19] Income Tax Regulations, Art. 109.
[20] Ibid., Art. 136.
[21] Ibid., Art. 125.
[22] Ibid., Art. 126.

curred must be charged to the new structure.[23] This is the same as under law of 1909.[24]

Incidental Repairs

These should be deducted as expenses.[25]

Depreciation Reserve

The depreciation reserve must be employed only for making good, losses on the property for which it was created. If the reserve exceeds the required amount it should be restored to income.[26] If any part of it is used for another purpose, income must be correspondingly increased.[27]

The advisability of restricting the use of the depreciation reserve to the renewal of losses on property for which it was created, might be questioned. It is clear, however, that the purpose of this clause is to prevent the employment of the reserve for purposes altogether foreign to that for which it was intended, making its legitimate use impossible.

Bonds

If a corporation purchases bonds above par it may deduct from gross income an amount proportionate to the life of the bond, providing this amount is written off on the books so that the book value will equal redemption value when the bonds fall due. The amount of the amortization must be proportioned with respect to three things: (1) purchase price, (2) maturity value, and (3) time of maturity. When bonds are issued below par, and must be redeemed at par when they mature, the loss thus sustained by the issuing corporation should be prorated over the life of the bonds.[28] Treasury Decision 1742 also permitted

[23] Income Tax Regulations, Art. 127.
[24] Treasury Decision 1742.
[25] Income Tax Regulations, Art. 131.
[26] Ibid., Art. 132.
[27] Ibid., Art. 133.
[28] Ibid., Art. 135.

annual additions or deductions for stocks under the law of 1909. These are discussed under the "Sale of Capital Assets" on page 89.

Patents

The investment in patents is made up of the cost of obtaining them—fees, drawings, models, etc. Since patents are monopolies granted for a period of seventeen years, the amount of the deduction allowable for depreciation of patents should be one-seventeenth of their actual cash cost. If the patent is bought outright, the price paid therefor represents its cost. If paid for in securities, then the actual cash value of the securities given is its cost.[29] If a patent becomes worthless before the end of the seventeenth year, that part of its cost not yet deducted may be deducted from gross income in the year in which the fact of such worthlessness is discovered, and such unreturned value shall be such part of original cost as the remaining number of years the patent has to run is part of seventeen years.[30]

Timber Land

The purpose being to return to the corporation an amount which, added to salvage value of land, will equal the amount actually invested, corporations owning timber lands and disposing of their timber will be allowed such amounts for depletion as will secure to themselves their original investment.[31] Further deductions are not allowable after an amount equal to the investment less salvage has been returned.[32]

Natural Deposits, Coal, etc.

Depreciation must be based on actual cost of such de-

[29] Income Tax Regulations, Art. 137.
[30] Ibid., Art. 138.
[31] Ibid., Art. 139.
[32] Ibid., Art. 140.

posits. Treasury Decision 1742 instructed corporations to value their deposits of minerals, etc., as at January 1, 1909, not on the basis of ordinary selling value less whatever it might cost to do the mining, as was done in Stratton's Independence, Ltd., *v.* Howbert, but on the basis of salable value of the entire deposit—*en bloc*—as at that date. Whatever the unearned increment at that date might be, it was to be excluded from the item of gross income. Therefore, if additional minerals are discovered later, investment cost may be returned before such additional minerals are exhausted. Further deductions should then be discontinued. The unearned increment is altogether neglected by the later regulations for the income tax.[33] When the mines are operated on a royalty basis no deductions can be claimed for depreciation.[34]

[33] Income Tax Regulations, Art. 146.
[34] Ibid., Art. 145.

CHAPTER VIII

VALUATIONS

State's Relation to Industry

Today the valuation of the properties of public service corporations for purposes of rate-making, purchase, taxation, and capitalization constitutes an important function of commissions and courts. Industries that are clothed with a public interest are now placed in a separate category, although their complete legal status does not appear as yet to be definitely outlined. Some fundamental distinctions exist between them and ordinary private enterprises, which necessitate considerable governmental supervision of the former. The interest of the public is directly involved—consequently the need of safeguarding it by some form of state control.

The past few years have witnessed a remarkable change in the relation existing between the State and these public utilities. It was formerly thought that competition was the essential regulating factor in all instances; but monopoly is now recognized as a permanent and unavoidable condition with which the Government must deal. Where conditions are favorable, competition affords the needed forces for the equitable adjustment of rates. Where rates are exorbitant, competition lowers them or else eliminates those who are unable to sell at normal prices. But in the absence of competition the regulative function is more and more coming to be performed by the State.

Recent Industrial Changes

Fifty years ago many of the modern industrial institutions were either unknown, or so new that their real position in relation to the consumer was not fully appreciated. Transportation facilities were so needed that franchises, grants, and privileges were given without any great amount of reflection upon the ultimate effect of such action upon the community. However, with the great industrial development of recent years, the growth of cities, the alterations in industrial and commercial methods, and the consequent changes in economic theory in conformity with these newer conditions, it has been found necessary to scan carefully the State's relation to industry, with the result that today the control of public utilities by the State is universally recognized as one of its legitimate functions. This interference finds points of contact in the State's power to tax and to determine an equitable charge for the services which the various public utility corporations render.

Taxation of Public Utilities

Taxes are essential to the existence of government and should be equitably borne by the property whose existence is made possible and perpetuated by the protective agency of the State. Assessments and valuations are made to enable the State to levy taxes, which are just in proportion to the State's ability to determine the equitable basis of computation. The problem is always difficult because of the difficulty of judging property values, both tangible and intangible. The work of valuing public service utilities is peculiarly difficult because of the complex character of their physical make-up, the difficulty of accounting for intangible values and of giving due weight to depreciation, the unearned increment in increasing land values, etc.

Public Utility Service

Public utilities affect the welfare of the people whom

they serve, through quality and kind of service offered and charges demanded. Usually they possess monopolistic franchises granted by the State or municipality. Oftentimes they are exclusive producers of a service because an attempt to duplicate this work results in disastrous competition, or is impossible. Two characteristics of public utilities—monopolistic form and extensive public service—make commission control desirable. Competition cannot act as a regulative force, since it leads to injurious rate wars and expensive duplication of works, thus sacrificing the interests of the public.

Public Service Commissions

The state railroad commissioners have shown the ability of the State to control, to a greater or less degree, an industry of a quasi-public character; while many states now have public service commissions which were formed by expanding the power and jurisdiction of existing commissions, or were newly erected by legislative enactment. They are clothed with plenary powers of regulation and ratemaking over the various public service corporations engaged in the telephone, telegraph, street railway, water and gas supply businesses, collectively known as public utilities, and adapted to control by commission for the reasons noted.

Growth of Commission Regulation

Already in several states the work of valuing both the physical and non-physical properties of public service corporations has been extensively undertaken. Principles governing all possible cases have not been finally promulgated, it is true, but much has been accomplished in the way of establishing sound rules of procedure. In many cases precedent is sufficiently strong and authoritative to make possible a statement of what may be expected to be the future policy. In other cases reports and decisions are conflicting, and the ultimate outcome must depend upon further elucidation of the matter or upon the decision of the Supreme Court of the United States—or both.

Massachusetts took the lead with the formation of a board of railway commissioners and with the organization in 1885 of a gas and electric light commission, while the control of telegraph and telephone companies was placed in the hands of a board of highway commissioners. Corporate capitalization and the issuance of securities have occupied chiefly the attention of the Massachusetts commissioners. Valuation for rate-making was exhaustively made by the Minnesota Railroad and Warehouse Commission, created in 1899, while the Railroad Commission of Texas, organized in 1891, has sought to ascertain the reconstruction value of the railroad bed, track, depots, and transportation facilities belonging to the railroads in the state. In 1907 New York established two public service commissions, having control of railroads, and electric and gas public service utilities. The Public Service Commission for the First District has jurisdiction in Greater New York, while the other has control over the remainder of the state, including telephone companies within New York City. In 1905 Wisconsin placed the control of express companies in the hands of her Railroad Commission, and later placed under its control practically all other public service corporations, thus transforming it into a full-fledged public service commission. Many other states have followed the example of these and the principle of commission regulation is fully established.

The Valuation Problem

It can be definitely stated that a differentiation must be made among valuations for different purposes, such as rate-making, purchase, etc., but it is sometimes difficult to say just how the differentiation should be made. Just what values ought to be excluded in one case or included in another, is a concrete problem that can be solved only in connection with the circumstances of each individual valuation. Taxation valuations must not be confused with valuations for purposes of capitalization, or valuations for rate-making. In Texas a valuation was made of the physical property of railroads for taxation purposes, but the Supreme Court of the United States declared that the results could not be used for rate-making because the basis of valuation was too narrow to comprehend all the elements of value.

It is often admitted that tax values of physical property ought to be stated below capitalization values, to prevent overtaxation of tangible property; and it was recently disclosed that St. Paul tax values equal about 60% of normal selling prices.[1] One public service commission states that its findings for capitalization purposes are not intended for rate-making purposes.[2] A corporation may perhaps hold assets for speculation, but not employ them in providing its customary services to the public. Consequently the corporation may not be justified in including such property with that upon which it bases its rates, although it ought to pay taxes on it. Methods and results of one valuation may be useful in another, but a valuation must be made with a view to its particular object.

Depreciation in Valuations

It follows that, from the standpoint of valuation, certain factors may or may not be of weight. Depreciation is

[1] Supplement to the Annual Report of the Railroad and Warehouse Commission of Minnesota, Nov. 30, 1908, page 16.

[2] P. S. C. R. (First District, New York), *re* Reorganization of Metropolitan Street Railway Co., Case No. 1305.

an important factor in most valuations where physical property is under examination, and sometimes even in the case of intangible property. It would appear that the only question as to the inclusion or non-inclusion of depreciation is answered when we have determined whether items of a depreciating character are to be included or omitted. Is depreciation a condition whose weight is determined by the purpose of the valuation, or is it absolute and independent of the purpose for which the valuation is made? Evidently the latter, for although different estimates may be made of its amount, this is due to disagreement on the part of those who do the valuing. They attempt to discover, and perhaps disagree upon what all admit to be in fact the same.

This granted, the problem of depreciation remains the same under all circumstances, whether the valuation is for rate-making, taxation, capitalization, or purchase. Here depreciation means reduced service value, and is usually measured in terms of dollars and cents. It will be the same for each item, although items that are included in one case are properly omitted in another. The difference is not one of depreciation, but of the inclusion or exclusion of depreciating values.

Depreciation is an important factor in valuations. Its determination is a different problem from the ordinary one in depreciation—writing down assets and creating funds for their ultimate replacement. In valuations we seek present values—values of today—not a notation of depreciation over long intervals with a view to ultimate replacement. The worth of an asset at some particular time in its life has not much bearing on ultimate replacement. To create a replacement fund we need know only lifetime and replacement cost. Greater rapidity of depreciation may occur early or late; the replacement fund can nevertheless be formed by equal additions each year, or by greater or smaller additions during either the earlier or later years.

By this is not meant that these two phases of the depreciation problem are entirely separated from each other. Rather it is intended to show wherein they differ and afford opportunity for comparison. If the gradual progress of depreciation could be accurately measured and some system employed by which the costs of the increments to the replacement fund could be made exactly equal to the costs of the losses through depreciation, then the two problems of *valuations* and *replacements* would be reduced to the same basis. Nor is it intended to say that this is altogether impossible. But it must be borne in mind that the amount in the depreciation fund and the actual depreciation need not of necessity equal each other, and certainly in most cases where a fund is formed by any of the methods in vogue—sinking fund, reducing balance, etc.—they will not be equal.

Present Value vs. Cost of Reproduction

In all valuations the distinction must be made between cost or cost-to-reproduce on the one hand, and present value on the other. Usually the comparison must be made between cost-to-reproduce and present value, because original cost is in most cases difficult to learn. Could it be learned, it would not be just to utility companies to deduct depreciation from original cost to find present value, for this would be ignoring appreciation due to the unearned increment in land, etc. For purposes of replacement, however, original cost should serve as the basis for computation of the replacement fund.

That this is right the answer to the following proposition will indicate: A machine cost originally $100 and must be replaced after ten years, at which time an identical machine can be purchased for $150. Should the depreciation be reckoned on the basis of original cost or of replacement cost? It seems clear that original cost ought to be the basis. To use replacement cost as a basis would permit the amortization of $150, whereas only $100 was invested. It would be presumptuous to assume that the original machine, which cost $100, took on during its lifetime an additional $50 in value merely because it will cost $150 to replace it. This greater cost is due to the increase in labor cost, cost of iron, etc., which in no way affects the original machine except possibly for selling purposes—usually a remote possibility. The additional $50 put in the new machine is an increase in the investment and should be charged to betterments. That rates ought to be increased to permit a reasonable return on such increases in the investment, is granted; but the increases themselves should not be paid for by the consumers. Nor does this mean that increases in investment arising from community development, scarcity of land, etc., cannot be considered a part of the investment upon which a return may be allowed. It simply means that the consumer cannot be expected to furnish the investment, and in addition replace it and provide a reasonable return thereon out of his pocket.

By comparison of cost-to-reproduce and present value, the amount of depreciation is supposedly found, although this overstates depreciation if in cost-of-reproduction we include increased cost of replacing wasting assets. Such increase is not depreciation but additional investment, as shown in the preceding paragraph.

Present value plus replacement fund—if it exists—may not equal or even approximate cost-to-reproduce, although it is sometimes assumed that it does. It ought not if wasting assets can be replaced only at increased cost, which increase should be represented by additional investment.

Whether or not it does is of importance in making replacements rather than in making valuations. As stated in the Metropolitan reorganization case, the problem is not how to meet and provide for decrease in values, but what is the fair value of the plant at present.[3] Reserve funds may provide ultimate replacement even though capital remains impaired to a considerable extent in the meantime, which will occur unless the fund accumulates at least as rapidly as value disappears.

Depreciation as Affecting Basis for Rates

Depreciation is a factor which determines values, and consequently must be considered in fixing an equitable basis for rates. To appreciate the bearing which depreciation has in this matter it is necessary to keep in mind the significance of the several bases that have been advocated for the making of rates. These are: original cost, cost-to-reproduce, and cost-of-reproduction-less-depreciation.

By original cost is meant actual money investment at the time of acquisition and construction. Although this method has some desirable features, it is generally admitted that it cannot be adopted as a basis for rates. Good accounting seeks to preserve the original cost figures, but usually these are lost in the various processes of reorganization, consolidation, etc. If preserved, they should be used rather to assist in finding an equitable basis for rates, than in being made to serve as such a basis. Discussion centers chiefly about the cost-to-reproduce and cost-of-reproduction-less-depreciation methods.

Cost-of-Reproduction Basis

Cost-of-reproduction as a basis for rate-making has been and is still held to be the true basis upon which to

[3] P. S. C. R. (First District, New York), Case No. 1305, page 155.

determine rates. Those who uphold this method assert that a distinction must be made between the efficiency of a utility and its value when determined for purposes of sale; that so long as the service performed is equally good as when the utility was new, it is immaterial to the consumer what the extent of the depreciation amounts to.

That depreciation ordinarily bears little or no relation to efficiency is shown in Chapter V, "Depreciation and Efficiency." Depreciation means that the time of replacement is approaching, and consequently the total service value of the thing depreciated is less than when new. But its efficiency remains unimpaired, and sometimes even increases as the result of adaptation and adjustment.

One of the most ardent advocates of the cost-to-reproduce basis is A. C. Humphreys.[4] As an illustration he takes the ties of a railroad or the poles of a telegraph line. Assuming that these have an average life of ten years, and that one-tenth of the total number should be replaced each year, Mr. Humphreys says that it is maintained by some that the average age of the ties or poles taken together is five years, and that therefore 50% depreciation should be deducted from cost of reproduction to determine the proper basis for rates. Mr. Humphreys says that while such a statement may be correct as a question of averages, it is entirely without warrant as a basis for the deduction of 50% from the investment. Such a procedure, he says, is confiscation, depriving the investor of a return on one-half of his investment. Rather, the only thing which the customer is concerned with is the efficiency of the service afforded, and if this is kept at 100% there can be no reason for reducing rates.

Mr. Humphreys further suggests that if a deduction

---

[4] Depreciation: Estimated and Actual; Proceedings of the American Gas Institute, Vol. 8, Part 2, page 521.

must be made from original cost to cover depreciation such as cannot be avoided by adequate renewals, then an amount equivalent to such deduction ought to be added to the appraisal as an item of cost, just as interest during construction and other items of intangible character are included.

The reproduction-cost-new theory has been upheld by the following additional authorities: Wisconsin Railroad Commission in *re* City of Whitewater *v.* Whitewater Elec. Lt. Co., Dec. 16, 1910; *re* Columbus Ry. & Lt. Co. *v.* City of Columbus, Ohio, 1906; Massachusetts Joint Board in Massachusetts Appraisal of the New York, New Haven and Hartford Railroad, 1911; also by C. E. Grunsky in Appraisal of Public Service Properties as a Basis for the Regulation of Rates;[5] William J. Wilgus in Physical Valuation of Railroads;[6] and Henry Floy in Valuation of Public Utility Properties (1912).

Cost-of-Reproduction-Less-Depreciation Basis

The reproduction-cost-less-depreciation theory has been upheld by the following authorities: Oklahoma Supreme Court in *re* Pioneer Telephone & Telegraph Co. *v.* Westenhaver, Jan. 10, 1911; New York Public Service Commission, First District, in *re* Metropolitan Street Railway Reorganization, Feb. 27, 1912; and by the Supreme Court of the United States;[7] also by Robert H. Whitten in Valuation of Public Service Corporations, page 359, New York, 1912; and, most recently, by the Special Committee of the American Society of Civil Engineers in their tentative report on Valuation for the Purpose of Rate-Making.[8]

---

[5] Transactions of the American Society of Civil Engineers, Vol. LXXV, page 770.

[6] Ibid., Vol. LXXII, page 203.

[7] Knoxville *v.* Water Co., 212 U. S. 1; 53 L. Ed 371 (Jan. 4, 1909).

[8] See Engineering News, Jan. 29, page 226, and Feb. 12, page 350, 1914; also Report of the Special Committee to Formulate Principles and Methods for the Valuation of Railroad Property and Other Public Utilities, Dec. 1, 1913, page 49.

With reference to the statements made by the advocates of the reproduction-cost-new theory, the above-mentioned committee observes that these writers invariably ignore the fact that a depreciation allowance is a return of a part of the investment, and that when the investment is thus returned it does not constitute confiscation to make depreciated value the basis for rates. Nor, says this committee, do the rates necessarily decrease when depreciated value is made the basis. Although it is true that in case of a given property the amount applicable to dividends grows less as the property grows older, this is altogether proper; for a continually increasing amount of the investment has been returned to the investors, and has been used in making replacements and additions, or perhaps is temporarily placed in a depreciation fund, with the result that the entire original investment remains intact at all times.

The case for the cost-of-reproduction-less-depreciation theory is stated clearly by Mr. Whitten. He says that this early depreciation of possibly 15%, which we have called composite depreciation, is properly charged to earnings as it accrues. However, instead of being placed in reserve when it can never be used for the object for which it was intended, it should be used to reduce the capital to the permanent requirements of the business. While this is not done in practice, what amounts to very much the same thing is done; i.e., the funds are used in making additions and betterments. Again, Mr. Whitten suggests, that since the service of a public utility is a continuous one, and can be rendered only by a plant the parts of which inevitably depreciate, the investment cost must be assumed to be continuous; and while at first thought it may seem that a uniform investment cost can be secured only by assuming a uniform capital value, this would be true only so far as interest and profits are concerned, but would not give a uniform total investment cost. Investment cost consists not only of simple interest and profits on the investment, but also includes cost of necessary repairs, renewals, and replacements. Since this latter cost is greater in an old than in a new system, the investment cost must be equalized by making the charge for the interest and profits correspondingly less, which can be done only by decreasing the investment, using for that purpose the savings made during the early years when renewals are few.

Rates will not be reduced because of the depreciated value of the old plant, for with the increased expenditures for repairs, renewals, and replacements rates would otherwise have to be increased. This can be avoided only by reducing the capital, and consequently the charge for interest and profits. In this way investment cost and charge are made uniform.

Equitable Basis of Rate-Making

The division of opinion as to the proper basis for rate-making is partly due to the apparent conflict of interest between the public service corporations and the people. That there is an equitable ground upon which to base rates could hardly be questioned. Integrity of investment must be observed, and any system of valuation that leads to confiscation is unjust. Investors and the people are both subject to imposition. The investor should afford suitable service and the people should pay therefor a price sufficient not only to return to the investor his capital, or prevent it from wasting, but also to afford him ample reward for his work in addition to the normal rate of interest on his money. No investor could ask for more; certainly the people should not be compelled to pay more. If a portion of the capital is returned to the stockholders in the form of dividends or by returning a portion of the company's securities, it would not be just to include the amount of such amortization for valuation purposes. The suggestion of Humphreys—that so long as service is efficient it is not the concern of the public what the amount of depreciation may amount to, since the proprietors are under obligations to make all necessary renewals and replacements—does not appear very logical. Who can compel the stockholders of a utilities company to make further payments into the treasury after their stock is full paid? How else have replacements, too long deferred and unprovided for, been made than by the issue of bonds to secure the funds that should have been provided out of revenue, thus placing corporations under the permanent disability of large fixed interest charges?

Rates Not Made Lower When Investment is Reduced

Those who uphold the cost-new theory do so from the belief that if the cost-new-less-depreciation plan is adopted, the rates will be made lower. But such would be the case only for the corporation as a whole, not for the security holders, since a portion of capital has been amortized and therefore permanently withdrawn from the business. If, on the other hand, the amount representing this unavoidable depreciation is retained by being reinvested in the form of additions and betterments, the capital would remain the same. It would not represent an additional investment but merely a transfer of a portion of the capital from one form to another. Additional investments should come from the investors, not from the revenues of the company, and should be made out of net profits rather than from gross income before net profits are determined.

Valuations for Purposes Other Than Rate-Making

Valuations for rate-making at present occupy the public attention more than valuations for other purposes. Nevertheless other valuations are of great importance. No doubt the present valuation of railroads being undertaken by the Interstate Commerce Commission will be found useful for a number of different purposes, including rate-making, capitalization, and taxation.

In the Metropolitan reorganization case the valuation was for capitalization purposes. Here obsolescence or supersession as one phase of depreciation was considered, and the folly of retaining obsolete or obsolescent property at original cost figures was shown. Within a period of twenty years many miles of track, once constituting the most valuable lines, had fallen into disuse. One constituent company with outstanding bonds amounting to one million dollars par value could neither sell nor lease its track, nor get money to carry on operations. Obsolescence was well illustrated by the inefficiency of the horse car lines. These lines constructed eighteen years before valuation were said to have seventeen years of service remaining, although the system was in fact obsolete and impractical. According to testimony, a certain sum set aside or expended annually would furnish renewals indefinitely and keep up the old horse car system. But merely making provision for the up-keep of an old horse car road was in this instance not considered good business policy.

Failure to make provision for future replacement of existing equipment by more up-to-date equipment necessitated the issue of new securities for the purchase of electric equipment, and this resulted in overcapitalization. Values once amounting to many millions of dollars had ceased to exist. The company held that these values should not be written off because allowance had been made for developmental expenditures in certain rate cases, although no visible evidence thereof remained. But this was not a rate case. The question was, to what extent should securities be amortized; and the Commission rightly contended that securities held for property now non-existent should be amortized.[9] Nor is it probable that such non-existent values would have been granted a place as developmental expenditures in a rate case.

Inadequate Allowance for Depreciation

Various valuations made by commissioners indicate what inadequate steps are taken to forestall depreciation and obsolescence. In the Queens Borough Gas and Electric case,[10] the New York Commission for the First District found this situation: reproduction cost, $1,608,492; present value, $1,139,812; depreciation, $468,680. Depreciation due to wear and tear, or physical depreciation only, is indicated, no allowance being made for future abandonments or supersessions consequent upon discoveries, inventions, improved processes, or functional depreciation. The wide margin between reproduction cost and present value resulted largely from failure to establish adequate depreciation reserves.

Depreciation Found on Basis of Averages

Equipment, structures, material, etc., inevitably depreciate, and various methods have been employed to indicate the extent to which at a specified time depreciation has occurred. In Michigan and Wisconsin, where valuations were made by tax commissioners, estimates were made of the present value of each unit. In Michigan more than 40,000 freight cars were thus inspected. A more economical and more accurate method was employed by the Railroad Commission of Washington. Mortality tables of

---

[9] P. S. C. R. (First District, New York), Case No. 1305, page 159.
[10] P. S. C. R. (First District, New York), Order and Opinion of June 23, 1911.

structures, working upon the same principles as life mortality tables, were used. Experience shows that similar structures, units of equipment, etc., have a definite average lifetime. Thus the average life of freight cars is approximately twenty-five years, the cars losing on an average of about 4% of their value each year. By multiplying the age in years by 4, the percentage of value which has expired is ascertained. This is then subtracted from 100, the remainder showing what percentage the present value is of original cost. To make possible the employment of this method, date of construction and cost new must be known.

Appreciation

Appreciation occurs in certain classes of assets, and should be given due weight in valuations. The roadbed of a railway appreciates during the first few years, when it is necessary to make repairs on account of inequalities and defects resulting from sinking, sliding, etc., and these repairs are charged to operation, although they are really capital expenditures. Additions of earth and stone are required, and the roadbed slowly grows firmer and safer as the old material becomes more compact. Allowance may be made for this by entering the value due to adaptation and solidification under a separate head representing appreciation after operating begins.

The Minnesota Commission allowed over 10% of original cost for this item upon lines of the Northern Pacific aggregating over 1,500 miles; while upon lines of the Minneapolis Western Railway, with a mileage of 6.89 miles, it allowed but slightly over 1%. The difference in the two cases was due to the better seasoning of the roadbed of the Northern Pacific. The Washington Commission says that appreciation continues about five years, when the value of the roadbed is approximately 10% greater than when new.[11]

If we may believe the statement of the New York Commission for the First District, appreciation is a simpler matter, and more easily handled, than depreciation. It says that if property grows in value, the investor has no cause for worry; and if the State recognizes his right to a fair return upon the increased values, he is adequately protected. It is unnecessary, says the Commission, that the increase be represented by securities, and further that if earning power is present, the holder of securities receives an adequate return regardless of the amount of these securities. But can the matter of securities be so lightly brushed aside? It may be true that, as was stated by the Railroad Securities Commission, the amount of the stocks and bonds is a matter of historical importance only, and par value is not a measure of actual value. But does this mean that the amount and par value of the securities are matters of no consequence? From the accountant's standpoint, the amount and par value of the securities present several considerations of the utmost importance.

In Smyth *v.* Ames,[12] the Supreme Court of the United States held that, to ascertain the fair value of a property, among other things to be considered are the amount and market value of its stocks and bonds. Certainly market value of stock does afford a basis for judging value, even though par value does not.

Recent valuations have done much for our enlightenment on depreciation in its various phases. Consideration of its principles in the work of valuation has indirectly shown the need of more scientific accounting, such as the

---

[11] Finding of Fact by the Railroad Commission of Washington Relative to the Valuation of Railroads, page 164.

[12] 169 U. S. 466.

establishment of adequate reserves for replacements; and the result of neglect and carelessness in this matter has been shown. Much remains to be done in the way of removing doubtful matters from their present tentative situation.

CHAPTER IX

LAND IN VALUATIONS

Land Not a Wasting Asset

Land, possessing some unique qualities, may be considered separately. It is not a wasting asset. Land normally appreciates, not through alterations in physical textures or arrangement, but because of scarcity, location, or the impossibility of duplication.

The wide variations in the results arrived at by experts in the valuation of land indicate the difficulty of the problem. The question of the unearned increment becomes of vital importance in public utility valuations, for upon the determination of the rightful owner of this increment must to a large extent depend the amount of the charges that may be asked. Under our present order of society this unearned increment belongs, rightly or not, to the fortunate possessor of land and may be regarded as a reward offsetting misfortunes in other directions. Nevertheless, there is a noticeable tendency to limit the amount of the rates that may be based on the unearned increment in the case of public utilities. Such limitation will presumably find its compensation in franchise privileges, monopoly, and right of eminent domain.

Land Values That May be Included

Whether or not land and appreciating land values ought to be considered in valuations depends on the purpose of the valuation. Where a public utility corporation possessed several tracts of land, it was held that only those actually and necessarily devoted to public use could be included for rate-making purposes. This despite the fact that rising land values may make it wise for the utility corporation to purchase lands that may not be "used and useful" in its service to the public for some time to come. The situation may justify such a purchase, but not the inclusion of the value thereof for rate-making, although it ought to be included in values for taxation.

Attitude of Courts

We have the authority of the Supreme Court of Minnesota in Steenerson *v.* Great Northern Ry. Co.,[1] that a railroad is entitled to earn a fair return on the cost of reproduction of its property; also the authority of the Supreme Court of the United States in Willcox *v.* Consolidated Gas Company, that, if property legally entering into the consideration of the rate question has increased in value since acquisition, the company is entitled to the benefit of the increase; adding, however, that this is the general rule, and that there may be exceptions where the property may have increased so greatly in value that a rate affording a reasonable return upon such increased value may be unjust to the public. (212 U. S. 19.)

Attitude of Interstate Commerce Commission

Thus there appears to be a limit to the growth of values upon which a public service corporation is entitled to what is called a fair return. There is a common tendency on the part of courts and commissions to place a limitation upon increasing values for rate-making purposes. The Interstate Commerce Commission faced this question in its investigation of advances in rates by carriers in western trunk line territory.[2] Railway officials declared that they

[1] 69 Minn. 353 (1897). The same attitude is taken in the more recent case of Shepard *v.* Northern Pacific Ry. Co., 184 Fed. 765 (1911).
[2] Opinion No. 1509, decided Feb. 22, 1911.

possessed a "legal right" to a fair return, not on the original investment, but on the estimated present value, resulting largely from increase in land values and amounting to many millions of dollars. Admitting the great services of the railroad to the State, the Commission asked whether larger income should not be derived from increased traffic rather than from heavier tolls on those already served. Public service corporations do business with the expectation of deriving an income from services rendered to the public, not from investments in land whose value happens to be increasing. Whatever may be the true economic or legal view on the right of a carrier to earn a reasonable return on the increased value of its land, says the Commission in substance, such an increase does not of itself afford the basis for an increase in rates upon a given service. This may be interpreted as leaving the question unsettled, since average rates may be made to furnish a fair return on increased values even though certain specific rates do not.

Attitude of Minnesota Commission

It is the belief of the Minnesota Railroad and Warehouse Commission that if railroads are permitted to realize on continually increasing land values by employing them as a basis for computing returns, they will ultimately absorb a disproportionate share of the country's wealth.[3]

Unusual Interpretation of Cost-of-Reproduction

The cost-of-reproduction method of valuing land has on certain occasions been given an unusual interpretation. Railroad officials have argued that land owned by their companies ought not to be valued at present market value, because the railroads, were they actually to buy the lands, would pay more than market value. So this additional cost

---

[3] Supplement to Annual Report, Nov. 30, 1908, pages iv-v.

is added to market value to determine cost to replace. That railroads do pay exorbitant prices for land is well known. This is because of injury resulting to contiguous property, and because land owners sometimes look with disfavor upon the projected road and take the opportunity to fleece the company.

If land is valued on this basis, a certain multiple of market value must be taken to arrive at reproduction cost. In Minnesota, investigation of a section of the Illinois Central indicated that of 35% of the right of way secured by condemnation the company paid about 4½ times average true value, while of the 65% purchase by agreement the price was 1.7 times average true value. Terminal lands in St. Louis cost 1¾, in Minneapolis 1⅗, and in Duluth 1¼ times normal value.

But when allowance has been made for actual excessive cost of land to railroads, it does not necessarily follow that they may write up these lands by the same multiple above *present* market values. Value as utility may be a more important consideration than reproduction cost in some cases, and, for rate-making purposes at least, extremely high valuations of property cannot be accepted merely because it could not be reproduced, or, if it could, only at very high prices. To establish original cost the railroad multiple should be used; also to establish cost of reproduction, and appreciation. But full cost of reproduction may not be allowed as a basis for rates.

Sales Method

The so-called "sales method" of determining present value has its uses and limitations. It is based on the assumption that as the assessed valuation of surrounding properties is to real value, so the assessed value of the property in question is to its real value. Thus, if land in a city is assessed at 60% of selling price, and a railroad buys 40 acres of land within the city limits for $12,000, the same land being assessed at $6,000, then the normal selling value would approximate $6,000 ÷ .60, or $10,000. So the railroad paid $2,000 above normal. The efficacy of this method is dependent on two conditions: (1) a sufficient number and variety of transfers to afford an accurate statement of average values, and (2) the equity of the assessed valuations. But inequality of assessment is notorious, and it seems that the method can be employed only within rather narrow limits and then may well be checked up with any other available information concerning the property in question.

Allowances to be Made

The special committee on valuation of the American Society of Civil Engineers believes that the present value of the land ought to be based upon actual cost plus subsequent appreciation. This appreciation is to correspond to that of surrounding property; and if the valuation cannot be made in this way, the land is best valued on the basis of current prices of neighboring land of similar character, increased by the ratio ordinarily existing in that section between land bought by public service corporations, and that purchased by private parties. Furthermore, the land is to be subject to the value of improvements existing upon it when it was purchased, such improvements to be valued at current prices.[4]

Appreciation Considered as Income

The appreciation of land values is apt to be considered in the same light as is depreciation of other kinds of assets. The United States Circuit Court in Consolidated Gas Co. *v.*

---

[4] Report of the Special Committee, page 52.

City of New York[5] in considering this matter says that appreciation and depreciation should be considered alike, and in expanding upon this principle the New York Public Service Commission, First District,[6] says that the only difference is that while depreciation is a loss to be debited, appreciation is a profit to be credited, since it represents an increase in assets. The Commission thinks that if land is taken at its depreciated value when it has depreciated, it is only fair to take it at its appreciated value under opposite conditions. To accomplish this it is suggested that an entry be made in the estimated receipts equal to average annual appreciation; otherwise, while the consumer is burdened with the depreciation of all other items, he will not receive any benefit from the appreciation of the land.

Appreciation Limited by the Supreme Court

Justice Hughes, in delivering the opinion of the Supreme Court of the United States, June 9, 1913, in the Minnesota Rate Cases,[7] apparently upholds the stand taken by the Interstate Commerce Commission in the railroad rate cases already considered. Declaring the cost-of-reproduction method inapplicable in the case in hand because of the conjectural results that would be secured, he asks whether in determining the fair present value of a railroad company's property as a basis for rates it is proper to value its right-of-way in excess of the market value of contiguous property similarly situated, i.e., whether such an increment of value is to be added as will not only cover increase in value resulting from the activities and prosperity of the community, but will constantly outstrip such increase in all neighboring lands.

[5] 157 Fed. Rep. 855.
[6] *Re* Gas and Electric Rates of the Queens Borough Gas and Elec. Co., 2 P. S. C. R. (First District), June 23, 1911.
[7] Simpson *et al.* *v.* Shepard; Same *v.* Kennedy; Same *v.* Shillaber; 230 U. S. 352.

The court concludes that the increased valuation to be permitted should not exceed average normal increase of other land in the community.

Old vs. New Value

It has been suggested that land acquires a special value by reason of the fact that it is peculiarly adapted to railroad or other public utility use. In such cases the question arises as to whether the owner of such land should receive compensation for the land on the basis of its value to him, or on the basis of its value in its newer function. On this point the United States Supreme Court maintains that it is the fair market value, the value lost by the owner, rather than the value gained by the taker that must be accepted.[8] This is no doubt the best policy to be pursued, since the added value is secured only as the result of the operations of the utility buying it.

Reproduction Method Employed on Lehigh Valley Railroad

Although the reproduction-cost theory for land has not been accepted by the Supreme Court of the United States, it has served as the basis for the valuation of the Lehigh Valley Railroad recently completed for the company. In this case three methods were considered: original cost; basic cost with no added cost for damages; and reproduction cost. Original cost was rejected as impossible because of faulty records. Basic cost, or cost based on average normal worth of neighboring tracts, was rejected as being inequitable. The reproduction method was adopted and resulted in an addition of 50% to the basic value of the road, which was believed to be a fair estimate of the reproduction cost of the road.[9]

---

[8] Minnesota Rate Cases, 230 U. S. 352.
[9] Engineering Record, May 16, 1914, Vol. 69, page 555.

Land Not "Used and Useful"

Many public utility corporations own land which, although it may be necessary for the future expansion of the plant, is for the present unnecessary for the service of the public. As a general rule the courts refuse to include the value of such land in the valuation of the utility's assets, on the ground that a fair rate should be earned only on the property "used and useful" to the public. It is evident, however, that to follow such a rule in letter rather than as a broad general principle, might lead to results exactly opposite those sought in so limiting the earnings of the company. Wherever such utilities have occasion to operate, particularly if they have prospects of future expansion, land appreciates rapidly in value; and to throttle the expansive power of the company by making it unprofitable to acquire additional land in anticipation of future growth, may tend to make rates higher when the land is ultimately purchased from necessity, than if the corporation had been granted a greater degree of liberty at an earlier period.

Too great freedom might lead to speculation, so that in this matter the attitude of the courts should be one of guarded leniency, granting to corporations a return on such unused property as will be needed to meet estimated future requirements. On the other hand, any income from such lands as are not in the public's service should serve as an offset to the amount of the fair return on such property which the public must pay; and any profits made by the sale of any such lands should be treated likewise.

Part III—Determining the Depreciation Charge

CHAPTER X

METHODS OF DEPRECIATION

Depreciation as Affected by the Point of View

The chapters which follow[1] describe the various plans that have been and still are advocated as valuable aids in the determination of the depreciation charge. Only after having secured an understanding of the principles employed in any method can its real significance be realized, and only thus can we place ourselves in a position to pass a rational criticism upon the different methods. For this reason more space has been given to their consideration than might otherwise have been necessary. The whole question of method has become so confused in the contest between conflicting views and opinions that it merits the most careful consideration.

Oftentimes obscurity results from inability to keep definitely in mind the full significance of the thing for which we are striving. The question of depreciation is chiefly concerned with two things:

1. The determination of the *cost* of maintaining the investment, which in turn is dependent upon—
2. The extent to which the investment has depreciated as the result of wear and tear, or other physical decay, or of obsolescence or inadequacy.

The cost of maintaining the investment may in turn be

[1] Chapters XI-XVI.

regarded as one of the elements entering into the cost of the output, either service or commodity, along with labor, fuel, and so on.

In valuations the question of depreciation is not essentially different, the difference being one rather of viewpoint than one which affects the fundamental problem itself. In valuations attention is directed rather to the extent of the depreciation at a point in time, for the purpose of determining value *at that time,* while from the other standpoint, depreciation *over a period* is the more important consideration. Valuations are made, for instance, to determine whether the owners of the property are securing an adequate return on their property at the time of valuation. This is the viewpoint of the Public Service Commission, which touches upon a corporation's affairs only at intervals, and somewhat as an external, supervisory agent. From the viewpoint of the company officials, on the other hand, depreciation is a constantly accruing expense, to be as constantly refunded out of the revenues of the business.

Cause and Effect

When the character and extent of an occurrence is determined by the operation of one or more agencies or forces, it is said to be functioned, or dependent, upon such agencies or forces. As the temperature falls, a steel rail contracts slightly; therefore its length, within certain limits, is functioned upon the temperature. Similarly, the accumulations of a sinking fund are functioned upon (1) the amount of the contributions to the fund; (2) the rate of interest; (3) the time during which the sinking fund accumulates; (4) the frequency with which interest is compounded. Likewise, the extent to which an investment in an industrial plant depreciates is functioned upon (1) the wear and tear; (2) obsolescence, arising from the possibility of displacement;

(3) inadequacy to perform its work, etc. Depreciation is not functioned upon passage of time but is merely conveniently measured in terms of time. Thus we say that in 5 years a plant depreciates 20% of its cost price. We use periods of time as a convenient way of comparing the rapidity of depreciation with the rapidity with which other occurrences coming within our experience take place. Without the action of such agents as wear and tear, obsolescence, or inadequacy, the investment would not depreciate at all.

Great Accuracy Impossible

The effects of past wear and tear, obsolescence, and inadequacy can be ascertained within reasonably narrow limits. The future effects of wear and tear, although they cannot be anticipated with entire certainty, may also be estimated, from experience, with a reasonable degree of certainty. Oftentimes even inadequacy may be foreseen, though usually with a smaller degree of certainty than wear and tear, because it is sometimes functioned upon unforeseen changes, such as movements of population, changes in demand, etc. Obsolescence can be predicted with perhaps even less certainty. It is notable, however, that although individual occurrences of a given character transpire apparently with entire uncertainty as to time, when large numbers of such occurrences are studied they may be found to follow a law. Thus the length of an individual life is altogether uncertain. Yet when considered in large numbers it is discovered that the span of the average life is calculable with enough accuracy to serve as a basis for the science of life insurance.

Much of the same thing is true of the items that compose an industrial plant, although it might not be profitable to carry the analogy too far. Mortality tables of structures have been used, and still greater accuracy may be expected as the result of longer experience. It will therefore be possible to gauge physical decay with reasonable accuracy, while obsolescence and inadequacy may be covered by a reasonable allowance in the nature of insurance over and above that for physical depreciation, or by being met when the exigency occurs, by writing off extraordinary losses, due to such causes, over a brief period of years. The necessity of this is apparent, for unless the investment indicated on the books is reduced to correspond to actual reductions in values through obsolescence or inadequacy, it will be impossible to meet the competition of more efficient plants and continue paying a normal rate of dividends.

The Straight Line Method

The simplicity of this method of determining depreciation (Chapter XI) stamps it with the appearance of practicability. It is free from interest complications, and its employment does not require a knowledge of the logarithmic or any other method of finding roots and powers of numbers. Speaking generally, there appears to be no reason why the straight line method does not approximate actual depreciation as nearly as any of the complicated curves at times advocated, apparently on the assumption that actual depreciation finds a counterpart in the accuracy of their mathematical computations.

It is not meant, however, to recommend unconditionally the straight line method. The question is one of expediency rather than accuracy; of expediency based on the principle that the interest of stockholders, bondholders, and the public must be diligently protected. To do this the procedure adopted should guarantee the return to the business through the rates charged, of an amount *approximately* equal to the expiration of plant values incident to the production of the commodity or service sold. It is axiomatic that depreciation is one of the costs of production, and hence a corresponding amount should be charged to gross income, and thus be retained to offset the exhaustion of capital.

The Reducing Balance Method

This method (Chapter XII) possesses the advantage of freedom from interest calculations, but, like any other method based on a fixed procedure, does not take into account either the actual rapidity with which depreciation occurs, or the various modifying factors which may show their influence at any time. Since this objection is common to all methods, other considerations will probably lead to a choice. Emergencies, such as rapid obsolescence, can in no case be foreseen; and the best that can be done is to alter the basis upon which future depreciation allowances are computed, changing the figures indicating value and remaining lifetime to conform to the altered conditions.

A glance at the table and Form 6 in Chapter XII shows what a preponderance the reductions for the first few years, for a property having a lifetime of 25 years, bear to those of later years. Such a rate of reduction must usually be out of all proportion to the actual rate of depreciation of the units of which an industrial plant is composed. From one point of view this is the method of extreme conservatism, since it writes down plant values far more rapidly than any other, and removes almost any possibility of a failure to set up adequate reserves. Usually the net result will be the formation of a secret reserve through the undervaluation of assets. Even if we assume the desirability of such a procedure, it may be questioned whether a new plant could bear the burden of the resulting heavy charges to revenue.

In an old plant the effects of the application of this method to many units of property of various values, lifetimes, and conditions, will tend to give a result of greater uniformity in proportion to the extent and variety of the plant; tending, however, to create a secret reserve measured by the excess of the actual value over the book value of the assets. It might be used to advantage in certain instances where obsolescence or inadequacy rapidly encroaches upon the property, although the accuracy with which actual depreciation would be covered would be at best approximate, and not gauged by the extreme accuracy with which the percentage on the reducing balance is calculated from the formula.

Interest

The interest question in depreciation has a twofold aspect. On the one hand, it has been asserted that the actual cost of an investment is not merely the bare original investment itself, but an additional amount represented by interest on the investment, since the money thus invested might have been loaned out on security at a fair rate of interest. This theory has given rise to the so-called "Annuity Method" described in Chapter XIV.

On the other hand, interest has been brought into the discussion of depreciation in connection with the establishment of sinking funds for the replacement of depreciated industrial plant. The "Sinking Fund" plan (Chapter XIII), and those which are based upon the sinking fund principle, viz., the "Equal Annual Payment" (Chapter XV) and the "Unit Cost" (Chapter XVI) plans, require interest calculations of this character.

The Sinking Fund Method

The persistence with which the sinking fund method has been advocated makes a careful consideration of it necessary. It is fully described and illustrated in Chapter XIII. The sinking fund formula provides a mathematically accurate method of accumulating a certain sum of money in a given time by means of equal periodic contributions permitted to accumulate at compound interest. Since such a fund grows not merely by the equal annual or other periodic additions made to it, but also by the interest accumulations of these additions, it follows that as the time during which the sinking fund accumulates is longer or shorter, so the portion of the entire fund formed exclusively by interest accretions will be larger or smaller. Thus, a fund of $100 accumulated in 25 years, interest at 5% by equal annual contributions, is composed of $47.62 interest accumulations and $52.38 direct contributions to the fund. For a shorter period the total interest accumulation would be less, and for a longer period greater, than that given above.

From this, one might conclude that the cost of creating a fund grows smaller with the increase in the number of years, since the total contributions necessary to secure a fund of $100 in 25 years on a 5% basis is only $52.38, while for longer periods it is yet smaller. The fallacy of this supposition is evident, however, if we remember that the equal periodic contributions to the fund are altogether withdrawn from the business, where they would have been employed at a profit, and that the longer such sums are held impounded in the fund, the longer the business is deprived of their use. Indeed, the business is not a very flourishing one if it cannot earn more by retaining these amounts in the business than can be secured in the form of interest accretions to them in a sinking fund.

The interest accumulations of a given year must be added to the annual contribution to the fund, to discover the actual burden for that year. Since the interest accumulations progressively increase, as may be seen by a glance at the table in Chapter XIII, the actual burden of the fund also increases yearly. In the foregoing illustration, it is more than three times greater in the last than in the first year.

There is no reason to suppose that depreciation increases at such a progressive rate. Moveover, the money should in most cases be reinvested in the business where it can be most profitably employed. The considerations which will make this plan the advisable one to follow must be such as are not usually confronted in practice. The seemingly great accuracy with which the calculations can be made, ought not to blind us to the essential phases of the plan.

Interest on Investment—Annuity Method

At first thought there appears to be some reason for including an allowance for interest on the depreciated investment, since the money thus invested would ordinarily produce an income when loaned on security, and without the risks incident to the investment. In reality, however, the net profits of business are usually composed of two parts not readily distinguished: (1) interest on the investment at say 2 or 2½%, about the rate paid on gilt-edge government bonds; and (2) over and above this, a reward for the extra hazards and risks of the business.

Briefly, a portion of the net profits represents interest on investment, and it would be a duplication of the interest charge to include it in the depreciation allowance. An inspection of the table in Chapter XIV will show that the total amount charged in the case of a $100 property with a lifetime of 25 years is $177.38, being made up of 25 equal annual charges of $7.0952. This is nearly twice the amount of the original investment, and the continued reservation of amounts on this basis would return not only the capital invested but a large additional amount, its magnitude depending on the interest rate and the lifetime of the property. This is equivalent to an actual reservation of profits, which, as is shown in Chapter IV. is not the purpose of the depreciation allowance.

There is yet another objection to this method. As the reader will see by an inspection of the table in Chapter XIV, and of Form 8, the equal annual charges are composed of both interest and depreciation charges, the depreciation charge increasing with, and being dependent upon, the decreasing interest charge. The depreciation charge is thus made the function of an assumed rate of interest, with the result that, in the case of the $100 property with a lifetime of 25 years, the charge for depreciation in the 25th year is $6.76 as contrasted with $2.10 in the first year. There would appear to be no reason whatever for such a procedure, for the property would, in theory, not only be required to pay a return on the remaining investment as at the beginning of the 25th year, amounting to $6.76, but in addition earn a sufficient amount during the year to amortize its entire value.

When one invests money in an industrial plant he expects a return equal to the ordinary rate of interest plus a reward for entrepreneur's profit, risk, etc. If money can be loaned on good security for 5%, by investing it in business one expects a return to cover not only interest which he might have received, but also an additional percentage for his extra labor and risk.

Should interest on investment be included in the depreciation charge, the balance of the revenue account will be correspondingly reduced, representing the gain over and above interest, or what may be termed extra-interest returns. If the money invested has been borrowed, and the same rate is allowed in the depreciation charge for interest as is paid on the money borrowed, then, providing the loan could be paid off as fast as the investment is reduced, the total charge for depreciation and interest on investment would be just sufficient to pay the loan and the interest thereon. Interest on borrowed money is a legitimate expense, but it should be considered under the head of interest, not of depreciation.

In a public utility whose rates are controlled by a commission, these rates are fixed to afford a suitable income; and since the investor cannot both loan his money on security and at the same time invest it in stocks, the most he can ask is a return equivalent to the ordinary interest rate, plus reward for hazard, etc. Therefore, if a deduction from income is made for interest on investment, rates cannot be raised to provide it again in the profits. If an allowance for interest on investment is made in the depreciation charge, it amounts to the retention of a portion of the profits in the business without recognizing them as such.

The Equal Annual Payment Method

Although an actual sinking fund is not created, this method employs the principles of the sinking fund to determine the depreciation charge, by making it what the charge for a sinking fund would amount to for the period in question, plus a sum representing interest on the remaining investment. This may be seen by examining the table in Chapter XV and comparing its contents with those of the table in Chapter XIII. The result is that if the rate of interest on the imaginary sinking fund is the same as that on the investment, an equal annual charge is secured exactly the same as that obtained by the annuity method, as indicated in column 6 of the equal annual payment table, Chapter XV, and column 5 of the annuity table, Chapter XIV. Moreover, since the sinking fund is entirely imaginary, there appears to be no objection to assuming the same rate of interest in both cases. When the interest rate on investment and in the imaginary sinking fund are the same, the net result of this plan in the illustration given is an excessive charge of $77.38, representing interest on investment.

If the interest on investment is placed at 7% instead of 5%, it amounts to $208.33 for an investment of $100, with a lifetime of 25 years—more than double the proper charge.

Instead of bringing the depreciation charge into as close correspondence as possible with the actual reduction of plant values, it is made a function of the growth of a sinking fund, and an imaginary one at that, based on an assumed rate of interest; and in order to make the charges equal they are increased by an imaginary return on the remaining investment, with the result that the equal annual charges are out of all proportion to the actual expiration of plant value. By carrying the items to the third or fourth decimal point, an appearance of great accuracy is obtained, which in reality bears little or no relation to the conditions to which it is intended to conform.

Undoubtedly it would be better to write down plant value by the sinking fund method than to make no provision whatever for depreciation. But we must remember that any depreciation charge based on purely assumed grounds may be considerably at variance from the actual conditions.

The Unit Cost Method

For valuations, especially where there exists obsolescence or inadequacy, this plan, as advocated, contains much that is suggestive, although vitiated by the introduction of the sinking fund principle. It is based on the fallacy that the sum of the annuities necessary to amortize plant value constitutes the total cost of amortization, and, in so doing, underestimates such cost by the amount of the interest accretions to the sinking fund. Since the interest accumulations form a smaller proportional part of short-time funds than of long-time funds, the net result of the unit cost formula is to underrate the value of the old plant, for in equation (3), Chapter XVI,

$$\frac{Q + P + F + iV}{Y} = \frac{q + p + f + iv}{y}$$

in which F represents the annuity to a sinking fund necessary to amortize V, the cost of the new plant, in N years, while f represents the annuity to a sinking fund necessary to amortize v, the depreciated value of the old plant, during its remaining life of n years. The left-hand term of the equation is assumed to represent the average unit cost of the product, or service, of the new plant; while the right side of the equation is assumed to represent the average unit cost of the product, or service, of the old depreciated plant. This is true in neither case, however, because F and f, the respective sinking fund annuities, represent less than the actual burden of the sinking fund, as has been shown; but since the lifetime of the old plant is usually less than that of the new one, the tendency is to understate the real cost of the burden of the new plant more than that of the old one, because the annuity constitutes a smaller part of the burden of a sinking fund over long periods than over short periods.

Thus, an annuity of \$2.0952 will accumulate, at an interest rate of 5%, to \$100 in 25 years; but $2.0952 × 25 = \$52.38, only a little more than one-half of the entire accumulation. On the other hand an annuity of \$18.097 will in 5 years, at 5%, accumulate to \$100, while the sum of the annual contributions will constitute far more than 52.38% of the total, or \$18.097 × 5, which amounts to \$90.485.

Each year's annuity to the 25-year sinking fund represents but little more than one-half of the average burden of the fund; while each year's annuity to the 5-year fund represents over 90% of the average annual burden of the annuity. The consequence is that, although cost of production is understated in both cases, it is understated to a greater degree in the case of a new plant than in that of a depreciated one. The net result, in the use of the formula given, is to understate the value of the old plant.

Actual Depreciation

In the illustrations of the different methods of depreciation in the following chapters, hypothetical cases have been assumed, in which plant value undergoes a gradual reduction from 100% to salvage value, or zero. However, in reality, an industrial plant, as a whole, does not depreciate in this way. In an extensive plant, value remains fairly fixed, beyond a certain unavoidable diminution during the first decade or so of its existence, resulting from the aging of the plant as a whole. This general aging is termed composite depreciation, and it amounts to possibly 15 or 20% of total value, neglecting improvements. After a certain point has been reached, however, depreciation and replacement become fairly complementary. Only in case of the replacement of an extraordinarily costly asset would its cost create an excessive burden on the revenues. In a less extensive plant, or one composed of a few very expensive properties, replacement burden, unless properly provided for, might at times be excessive, and even disastrously so, and a method of caring for such costs should be contrived which is sufficiently simple to be workable and at the same time accurate and inclusive enough to be valuable.

Such a method should not be based upon the cost and estimated lifetime of the entire plant, as this would make it impossible to give due weight to variations in the different units composing the plant. Average lifetime of a plant is too indefinite a basis, and makes impossible the proper allocation of the depreciation cost to the output of the machine or unit of the plant to which it is incident. In so far as any of the formal methods described in the following chapters are to be advocated, it should be understood that it is only as they apply to the units into which the plant can be divided most readily, and not to the plant as a whole, which is too complex to serve as a suitable base for calculating depreciation.

CHAPTER XI

THE STRAIGHT LINE METHOD

Characteristics

This is the simplest of the several plans that have been suggested to determine theoretical depreciation and make proper allowance for it in the records. It is based on the assumption that if the investment in dollars and cents is divided by the number of years, or periods, of the lifetime of a property, the resulting quotient expresses the amount in dollars and cents which should be allowed each year to cover accrued depreciation and prevent the lessening of invested capital. Whether the best method or not, it is at once the least complicated and most easily understood. No interest computations of any kind are involved, either on the investment itself, as in the annuity and equal annual payment methods, or on the annual allowances, as in the sinking fund method.

The Straight Line Formula

Having given the investment, lifetime, and salvage value of a property, let V represent the investment; n the lifetime in periods, as years or months; and V^1 the salvage value. Then if we assume x to equal the amount of the equal annual charges, an equation may be formed as follows:

$$(1) \qquad x = \frac{V - V^1}{n}$$

If salvage value is zero, then:

(2) $$x = \frac{V}{n}$$

Illustration of Straight Line Method

Assume the case of a plant costing \$100, having a lifetime of 25 years and a salvage value of zero. Substituting these values in formula (2), we have:

$$x = \frac{\$100}{25} = \$4$$

Four dollars, therefore, is the annual charge necessary to write off the investment in 25 years.

Straight Line Tabulations

The accompanying table shows in detail the accumulations of the charges when made on this basis, and also the reduced theoretical value of the remaining investment at the end of each year. It is so simple as to require no explanation, and is given partly to make the treatment uniform with that in the chapters which follow.

Graphic Illustration of Straight Line Method

Form 5 (see page 137) is a graphic illustration of the straight line method. The upward progress of the graph indicates value in dollars, while its progress from left to right represents time in years. Thus, at the end of the 10th year \$40, or 40% of the investment, has in theory expired, and has been charged off in the income account as an expense.

Straight Line Method

TABLE OF COMPUTATIONS

Age in Years	Value at End of Each Year	Depreciation During Year	Total Accrued Depreciation at End of Each Year
0	$100.00		
1	96.00	$4.00	$4.00
2	92.00	4.00	8.00
3	88.00	4.00	12.00
4	84.00	4.00	16.00
5	80.00	4.00	20.00
6	76.00	4.00	24.00
7	72.00	4.00	28.00
8	68.00	4.00	32.00
9	64.00	4.00	36.00
10	60.00	4.00	40.00
11	56.00	4.00	44.00
12	52.00	4.00	48.00
13	48.00	4.00	52.00
14	44.00	4.00	56.00
15	40.00	4.00	60.00
16	36.00	4.00	64.00
17	32.00	4.00	68.00
18	28.00	4.00	72.00
19	24.00	4.00	76.00
20	20.00	4.00	80.00
21	16.00	4.00	84.00
22	12.00	4.00	88.00
23	8.00	4.00	92.00
24	4.00	4.00	96.00
25	0.00	4.00	100.00
		$100.00	

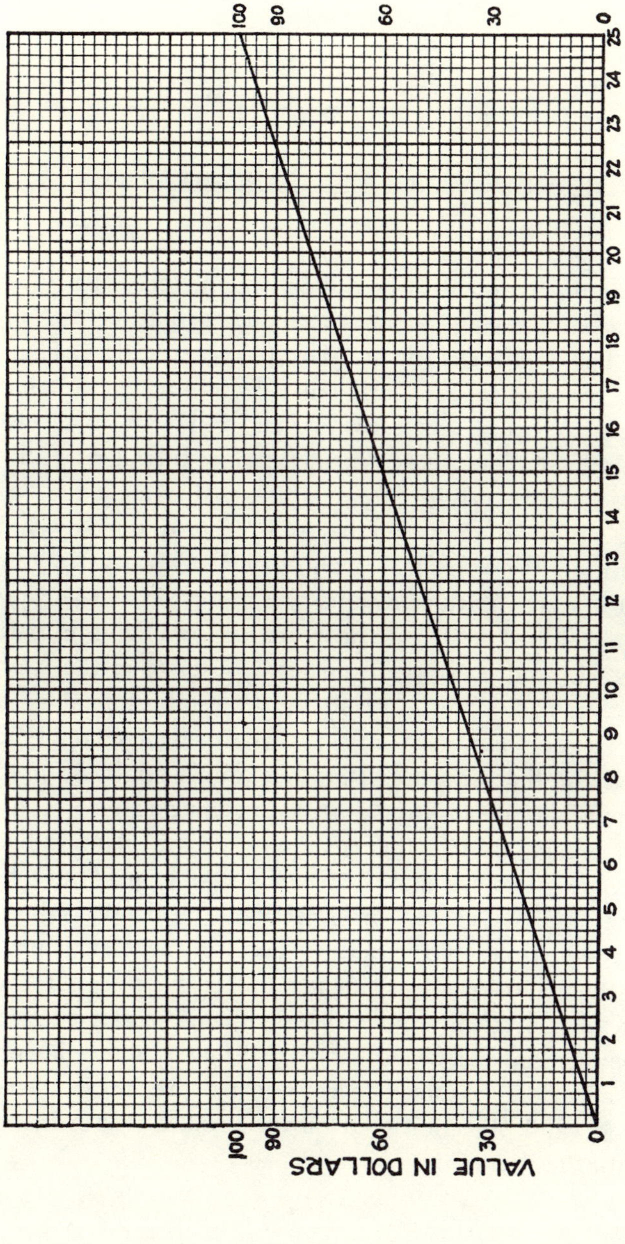

Form 5. Graphic Illustration of Depreciation—Straight Line Method

CHAPTER XII

THE REDUCING BALANCE METHOD

Characteristics

Assuming the plant to be a unit which depreciates from 100% value to salvage value, the reducing balance method requires heavy charges during the first years of the plant's lifetime, these charges continually decreasing in amount from year to year. Since repairs and renewals cost least during the first years, increasing with more advanced years, they offset, to a certain extent at least, this inequality of charges, and tend to make the total cost of up-keep and depreciation more uniform than would otherwise be the case. If it were desirable to amortize a portion of the capital as the result of composite depreciation, by buying in part of the stock, and there were no legal obstacle in the way, funds accumulated as the result of the establishment of a reserve larger than necessary for replacements could be employed for that purpose. Or such funds might be used for the purchase of additional plant to compensate for composite depreciation in other portions of the plant. The undetermined financial status of newly established concerns sometimes affords cause for objection to this procedure, since, as sometimes unfortunately occurs, expediency may compel the payment of dividends to the sacrifice of the reserves. Theoretically, however, dividends cannot be paid until depreciation has been allowed; so that if the reducing balance method is assumed to represent depreciation, there will be no valid objection to it on the ground that it interferes with the declaration of dividends.

The Reducing Balance Formula

The reducing balance plan charges off a constant percentage on the decreasing balance, beginning with the original investment and thus reducing it to salvage. This constant percentage must be such that at the end of a given number of periods, or years, the investment less salvage will have been written off. A formula for such a procedure will now be developed.

Assume that V^1 represents salvage value; V the original investment; n the number of periods, as years or months. Let the constant percentage necessary to reduce V to V^1 in n periods, by deducting for each period such percentage from the balance remaining over from the previous period, be represented by x. Since V represents the original value of the asset, then, theoretically, its value at the end of the first period will be $V(1-x)$. To illustrate, suppose we know that for a fixed number of years the percentage by which the balance must each year be reduced in order to reach salvage value in a stated number of years, is 37%, or .37 of the reducing balance. Deducting .37 of the balance from the reducing balance is equivalent to multiplying the balance by $1-.37$, or .63. Thus:

(1) $\$100 \times .37 = \$37;\ \$100 - \$37 = \$63$

(2) $\$100 \times (1 - .37) = \$63$

Since $V(1-x)$ is the first diminished balance, resulting from the deduction of the fixed percentage from the original investment, so $V(1-x)(1-x)$, or $V(1-x)^2$ is the diminished balance at the end of the second period, because $V(1-x)$, the balance at the beginning of the second period, must be reduced by the constant percentage, just as was V, the investment at the beginning of the first year, by multiplying it by $(1-x)$. $(1-x)$ therefore occurs twice as a multiplier, i.e., it is squared, and $V(1-x)(1-x)$ may be stated better as $V(1-x)^2$. At the end of the third period the balance must again be reduced by multiplying by $(1-x)$, and the resulting balance becomes $V(1-x)^3$. If n represents the given number of periods, then the balance at the end of the nth year will be $V(1-x)^n$, which, according to our assumption, must represent salvage value, or V^1. Put in form of an equation:

$$(3) \qquad V(1-x)^n = V^1$$

We can now find the value of x, the unknown percentage, in terms of the other quantities, all of which are known. Dividing both terms of the equation by V, which will not alter the equality, we get:

$$(4) \qquad (1-x)^n = \frac{V^1}{V}$$

Similarly we can take the nth root of both terms of equation (4) without altering the equality, thus obtaining:

$$(5) \qquad (1-x) = \sqrt[n]{\frac{V^1}{V}}$$

According to a simple algebraic principle the signs of both terms of equation (5) may be changed from + to — or from — to + and the equality still preserved, thus:

$$(6) \qquad (x-1) = -\sqrt[n]{\frac{V^1}{V}}$$

Lastly, the equality is still preserved if in changing any quantity from one side of the equation to the other we simply change its sign. Thus we may obtain:

$$(7) \qquad x = 1 - \sqrt[n]{\frac{V^1}{V}}$$

which states the value of x in terms of time n, original investment V, and salvage V^1.

Illustration of Reducing Balance Method

Assume the case of an imaginary plant costing $100, and depreciating in 25 years to a salvage value of $1. Further, assume that the depreciation occurring each year is a constant percentage of the balance of the investment remaining at the beginning of the year. The problem is to find this constant percentage. Substituting our values in formula (7) we have:

$$x = 1 - \sqrt[25]{\frac{1}{100}}$$

When solved the value of x is found to be .168236. The balance must therefore be reduced each year 16.8236%.

Reducing Balance Tabulations

In the table which follows are tabulated all the items in the problem, extending over a period of 25 years. The first column indicates the age of the plant; the second column the value of the balance at the end of each year, after having been reduced from the previous year by .168236; the third column each year's depreciation; while the fourth column shows the total accrued depreciation to the end of each of the 1-year periods. From this it is seen that over 50% has been written off in 4 years, and over 90% at the end of the 13th year, or when the plant has barely passed middle age. The charges for the last few years are insignificant compared with the first one.

Reducing Balance Method

TABLE OF COMPUTATIONS

Age in Years	The Reduced Balance	Depreciation for Each Year	Amount of Depreciation from Beginning to End of Each Year
0	$100.0000		
1	83.1764	$16.8236	$16.8236
2	69.1831	13.9933	30.8169
3	57.5441	11.6390	42.4559
4	47.8631	9.6810	52.1369
5	39.8108	8.0523	60.1892
6	33.1130	6.6978	66.8870
7	27.5422	5.5708	72.4578
8	22.9286	4.6136	77.0714
9	19.0712	3.8574	80.9288
10	15.8626	3.2086	84.1374
11	13.1939	2.6687	86.8061
12	10.9742	2.2197	89.0258
13	9.1280	1.8462	90.8720
14	7.5915	1.5365	92.4085
15	6.3143	1.2772	93.6857
16	5.2530	1.0623	94.7480
17	4.3685	.8835	95.6315
18	3.6336	.7349	96.3664
19	3.0223	.6113	96.9777
20	2.5139	.5084	97.4861
21	2.0910	.4229	97.9090
22	1.7412	.3498	98.2588
23	1.4483	.2929	98.5517
24	1.2046	.2437	98.7954
25	1.0018	.2028	98.9982
		$99.0000	

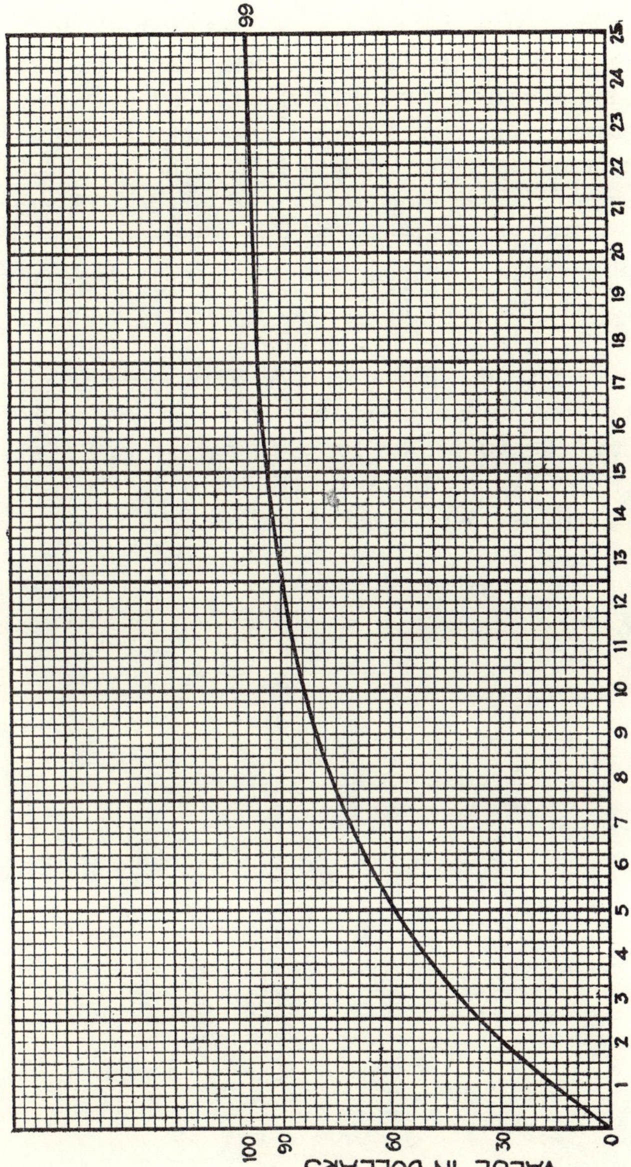

Form 6. Reducing Balance Curve (plotted from data in first and last columns of foregoing table)

Graphic Illustration of the Reducing Balance Method

Form 6 indicates graphically the facts given in the table. Vertical spaces represent values, and horizontal spaces time, as designated. The rise of the curve indicates the accrual of depreciation upon the reducing balance theory. In the table, accrued depreciation at the end of the 6th year amounts to $66.89. This may be found approximately in the graph by noting what amount in dollars is diagonally opposite the 6-year point in the rectangle one of whose upright sides is determined by the intersection of the curve with the vertical line drawn from 6. The exact amount in dollars is not likely to be found, as it is indicated at only five points, 0, 30, 60, 90, and 100, each vertical space representing $3. However, the amount indicated by the curve for any given time can be read approximately.

CHAPTER XIII

THE SINKING FUND METHOD

Characteristics

The sinking fund method derives its name from the fact that it employs the principles which are ordinarily used in the establishment of sinking funds for the liquidation of bonded indebtedness, as well as for purposes of replacement, etc. It might also be called the compound interest method, since sinking funds accumulate by compound interest, and because it is sometimes employed without establishing an actual sinking fund, as in the equal annual payment method, considered in Chapter XV.

We must not forget that where the rate of depreciation is made a function of a rate of interest, such depreciation is purely theoretical, and may or may not approximate actual depreciation. Some confusion has resulted from attempting to indicate depreciation by means of interest formulas, with the result that such methods have been branded by some writers as illusory, and misleading. The way to determine actual depreciation is by inspection. But this does not necessarily render useless, formulas which can be applied with due consideration of the facts in the case. The problem is one of expediency, and whatever plan will aid in a solution of the problem ought to be adopted. The possible usefulness of the various methods has already been discussed in Chapter X.

By the sinking fund method a fixed sum of money is placed aside each period and allowed to accumulate at compound interest. The amounts thus set aside, plus their interest accumulations, must be such as to equal the desired amount at the end of an assumed period. Although the annual charges remain constant, the actual burden increases each period, because in addition to the equal amounts placed in the fund periodically, there are the continually increasing interest accumulations which represent the earning capacity of the fund and which are not received through the usual channels of revenue as they would be if the funds were reinvested in the business.

The Sinking Fund Formula

Assume an imaginary plant with a value of $100, lifetime of 25 years, and salvage value of zero. Our problem is to find what sum of money must be set aside each year in order that at the end of 25 years the fund will have accumulated to $100, at 5% interest, compounded annually.

When a series of numbers increases or decreases by a constant factor, it forms a geometrical progression whose terms consist of the respective annual charges plus their interest accumulations at the end of the assumed period of years. In the problem given, it is evident that the last one of the 25 fixed payments will accumulate no interest, since it is made at the end of the 25th year, when the fund will be needed to make the desired replacement. The next to the last payment (24th) will accumulate interest for 1 year; while the one preceding this will accumulate not only 1 year's interest on the payment made to the fund, but also 1 year's interest on the sum of the 23rd payment after being enhanced by its first year's interest accumulation, and so on. 5% being the rate of interest, we obtain a series which increases by a constant factor (1.05), thus:

The last year the charge accumulates no interest, so it amounts to 1.00 times the charge.

Next to last year the charge accumulates to 1.05 times the charge.

Second year from the last, the charge accumulates to 1.1025 (1.05×1.05) times the charge.

Third year from the last, the charge accumulates to 1.157625 (1.1025×1.05) times the charge, and so on, each year's charge accumulating to an amount 1.05 larger than the amount accumulated by the charge of the year following.

Thus the constant factor is 1.05 in the series consisting of the annual charges plus their interest accretions. Now, if we assume x to be the fixed annual payment necessary to produce the required sum, then $x \times 1.05$ is the accumulation of the next to the last year's payment; $x \times 1.05^2$ that of the preceding year; $x \times 1.05^3$ that of the next preceding; and so on. In this instance, $x \times 1.05^{24}$ is the accumulation of the first payment invested. To secure a general formula let r represent the constant factor, and n the number of years. Then:

$$x + xr + xr^2 + xr^3 + xr^4 + \ldots + xr^{n-2} + xr^{n-1}$$

is the general form of the increasing geometrical progression. The sum of these terms, or V, must equal the fund accumulated after n years, by investing x dollars in a fund accumulating at the rate of r. This sum is a known quantity, being $100 in the problem assumed. By a well-known mathematical principle,[1]

$$(1) \qquad V = \frac{(xr^{n-1} \times r) - x}{(r-1)}$$

$$(2) \qquad \therefore V = \frac{(xr^n - x)}{(r-1)}$$

[1] To find the sum of the terms of a geometric series, multiply the greatest term by the ratio; from the product subtract the least term; divide the remainder by the ratio less 1.

$$(3) \qquad \therefore V = \frac{x(r^n - 1)}{(r - 1)}$$

$$(4) \qquad \therefore x = V\frac{(r - 1)}{(r^n - 1)}$$

Illustration of Sinking Fund Method

Substituting in equation (4) the values assumed above, and solving by logarithms, we have:

$$x = \$100\frac{1.05 - 1}{1.05^{25} - 1} = \$2.0952+$$

That this amount set aside each year, at 5% compound interest, for 25 years, will amount to $100, may be proven by using formula (3):

$$V = \$2.0952\frac{(1.05^{25} - 1)}{(1.05 - 1)} = \$100$$

Since in practice fractions smaller than one cent cannot be dealt with, the amount of each instalment would be $2.10. This, compounded at 5% for 25 years, would slightly exceed $100, and would amount to $100.22.

Sinking Fund Tabulations

In the table which follows, all figures secured in the solution of this problem are tabulated. The first column shows the age in years; the second column the value at the end of each year; the third column the equal annual payments to the depreciation fund; the fourth column the interest accumulations of the fund; and the fifth column the

SINKING FUND METHOD

TABLE OF COMPUTATIONS

Age in Years	Value at End of Year	Annual Payment to Sinking Fund	Annual Accretion of Interest in Sinking Fund	Actual Annual Cost, or Payment, Plus Year's Interest Accumulations
0	$100.0000			
1	97.9048	$2.0952	$0.0000	$2.0952
2	95.7074	2.0952	.1049	2.2001
3	93.3947	2.0952	.2148	2.3100
4	90.9693	2.0952	.3302	2.4254
5	88.4225	2.0952	.4516	2.5468
6	85.7483	2.0952	.5790	2.6742
7	82.9405	2.0952	.7126	2.8078
8	79.9923	2.0952	.8530	2.9482
9	76.9866	2.0952	1.0005	3.0957
10	73.6462	2.0952	1.1552	3.2504
11	70.2333	2.0952	1.3177	3.4129
12	66.6497	2.0952	1.4884	3.5836
13	62.8870	2.0952	1.6675	3.7627
14	58.9361	2.0952	1.8557	3.9509
15	54.7876	2.0952	2.0533	4.1485
16	50.4317	2.0952	2.2607	4.3559
17	45.8581	2.0952	2.4784	4.5736
18	41.0557	2.0952	2.7072	4.8024
19	36.0133	2.0952	2.9472	5.0424
20	30.7187	2.0952	3.1994	5.2946
21	25.1594	2.0952	3.4641	5.5593
22	19.3221	2.0952	3.7421	5.8373
23	13.1930	2.0952	4.0339	6.1291
24	6.7574	2.0952	4.3404	6.4356
25	0.0000	2.0952	4.6622	6.7574
		$52.3800	$47.6200	$100.0000

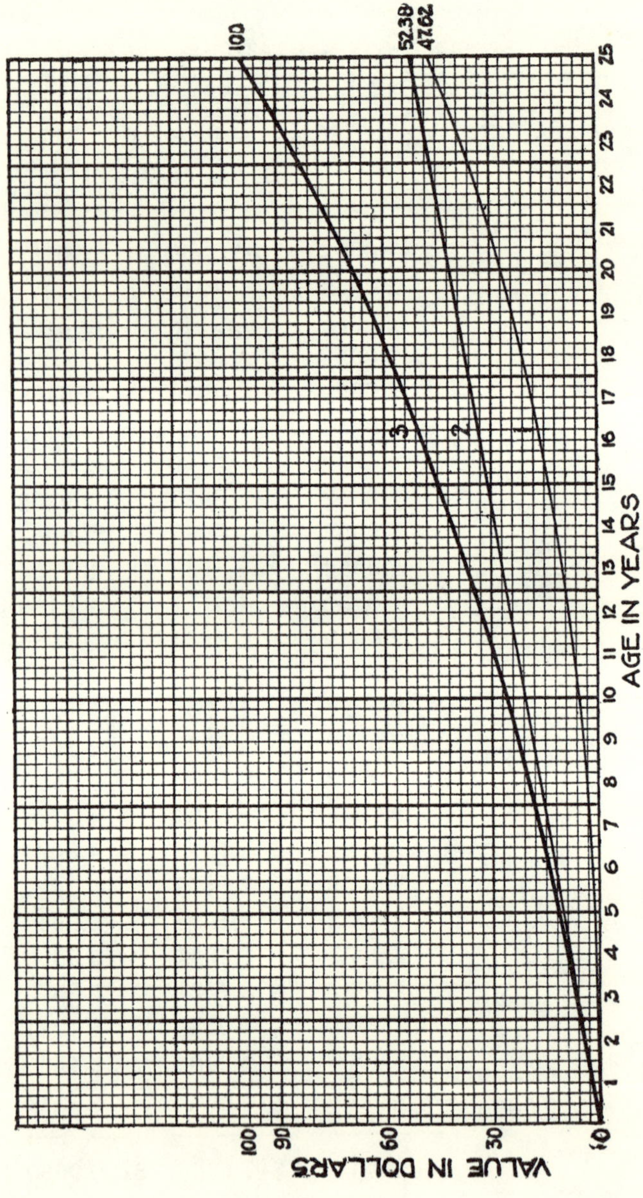

Form 7. Sinking Fund Curves (plotted from data on page 149)

actual burden for each year secured by combining the results in the third and fourth columns.

Graphic Illustration of Sinking Fund Method

The problem is solved graphically in Form 7. Curve 1 indicates the growth of the interest accumulations; 2 the equal annual charges (this is a straight line); and curve 3 the resultant of 1 and 2. Note that in this instance the interest accumulations, $47.62, are but slightly less than the payments to the fund, $52.38.

CHAPTER XIV

THE ANNUITY METHOD

Characteristics

This method bears some resemblance to the equal annual payment method (Chapter XV), as in both an allowance is made for interest on the investment remaining at the beginning of each period. Under the equal annual payment method the diminution of the investment is arbitrarily determined by assuming that the depreciation is equal to the gradual increase of a sinking fund based on a given rate of interest.

Similarly the annuity method proceeds on the assumption that interest on the remaining investment should be allowed for in the revenues; and also that the annual allowances should be equal, as is the case under the equal annual payment method when the rate of interest on the investment is the same as is assumed for the sinking fund.

Under the annuity method, however, the equal annual charge is determined without the assumption of any depreciation rate, by merely finding such a sum as, when deducted each year from the sum of the remaining investment and the interest thereon at a given rate, will write down the investment to salvage, or zero, and in addition return the full amount of the interest on the investment as it stands from beginning to end of the plant's life. Interest for the first year is on the original investment; for the second year on the original investment *reduced* by the amount that the total annual allowance for interest and depreciation is in excess of the interest on investment for the first year. Thus that part of the allowance covering the item of interest will gradually diminish, while that part covering depreciation will correspondingly increase, the two combined being always the same.

But, whereas under the equal annual payment method the amount of the depreciation, and consequently the remaining investment, depends upon the growth of a theoretical sinking fund, under the annuity method the controlling factor is the rate of interest on the investment. As the rate is lowered this method approaches nearer and nearer to the straight line method, becoming identical with it when the interest is zero. Under the equal annual payment method the depreciation is made a function of the rate of interest upon which a sinking fund accumulates, while in the annuity method the depreciation is a function of the assumed rate of interest on the investment.

The Annuity Formula

The annuity plan charges off an equal amount each year sufficient to cover interest on the remaining investment, and in addition to reduce plant to salvage, or zero, at the end of a given time. Let V represent original value, V^1 salvage value, n the lifetime of the plant, and r the rate of interest plus 1.

Since V is the original value, Vr, that is, V multiplied by 1 plus the rate of interest, is the sum of the original investment plus interest on it for the first period. For instance, if the original value is \$100, and interest on investment is computed at 5%, then \$100 $\times$ 1.05 (1 plus the rate of interest) equals \$105, or the original investment plus one year's interest.

If we let x represent the equal annual charge, the amount of which we are seeking, and which is just sufficient to return both principal and interest thereon at the given rate, then it is clear that the investment remaining after the first annual charge—and the investment at the beginning of the second period—will be $(Vr-x)$. Therefore, following the same procedure as before, the interest on the investment for the second period will be $(Vr-x)$ multiplied by 1 plus the rate of interest, or $(Vr-x)r$. From this in turn we deduct x, the second annual charge, which gives us the investment at the beginning of the third period, or $(Vr-x)r-x$, and so on for as many periods as necessary. Suppose the lifetime of the plant is four years, then:

(1) $$\{[(Vr-x)r-x]\,r-x\}\,r-x=V^1$$

Removing the first parentheses,

(2) $$[(Vr-x)r-x]\,r^2-xr-x=V^1$$

Removing the second parentheses,

(3) $$(Vr-x)r^3-xr^2-xr-x=V^1$$

Removing the last parentheses,

(4) $$Vr^4-xr^3-xr^2-xr-x=V^1$$

We next solve this equation for x, by first transferring Vr^4 to the opposite side of the equation, changing its sign, thus:

(5) $$-xr^3-xr^2-xr-x=V^1-Vr^4$$

Changing the signs of all terms we have:

(6) $$xr^3+xr^2+xr+x=Vr^4-V^1$$

Or,

(7) $$x(r^3+r^2+r+1)=Vr^4-V^1$$

Dividing both terms by (r^3+r^2+r+1),

$$(8)\qquad x=\frac{Vr^4-V^1}{r^3+r^2+r+1}$$

Or,

$$(9)\qquad x=(Vr^4-V^1)\frac{(r-1)}{(r^4-1)}$$

By substituting n for 4, a general formula is obtained, applicable to any number of periods, thus:

$$(10)\qquad x=(Vr^n-V^1)\frac{(r-1)}{(r^n-1)}$$

Illustration of Annuity Method

Assume an imaginary plant costing $100 and having a lifetime of 25 years. Assume further that the investment as at the beginning of each year should have a return of 5% thereon. Substituting these known terms in our formula we have:

$$x=100\times 1.05^{25}\,\frac{(1.05-1)}{(1.05^{25}-1)}$$

which when solved with the aid of logarithms gives $7.095245+ for the value of x; that is, the equal annual allowance that must be made to afford a return of 5% on the investment, and also reduce the investment to zero at the end of the 25th year. Since the investment gradually decreases, the theoretical depreciation gradually increases; the sum of interest on investment plus depreciation allowance being always $7.095245+. It should be noted that the same results are secured by this method as by the equal annual payment method when the rate of interest employed is the same as is used in the equal annual payment method, both for computing depreciation on a sinking fund basis and for computing interest on the investment.

Annuity Tabulations

The table which follows details the computations for the problem given above. The first column gives the age of the plant in years; the second column indicates the theoretical value at the end of each year; the third column gives the interest on the remaining investment each year; the fourth column gives the theoretical depreciation; and the items in the fifth column are formed by combining interest on investment and depreciation, which is the allowance for each year. The contents of the accompanying annuity table should be carefully compared with those of the equal annual payment table of Chapter XV.

Graphic Illustration of Annuity Method

This problem is illustrated graphically in Form 8. Curve 1 indicates the depreciation; curve 2 the interest on the investment; and the straight line 3 shows the resultant of curves 1 and 2.

Annuity Method

TABLE OF COMPUTATIONS

Age in Years	Value at End of Year	Interest on Remaining Value of Property at 5%	Combined Depreciation Allowance	Depreciation Plus Interest on Investment
0	$100.0000			
1	97.9048	$5.0000	$2.0952	$7.0952
2	95.7047	4.8952	2.2001	7.0952
3	93.3947	4.7852	2.3100	7.0952
4	90.9693	4.6697	2.4254	7.0952
5	88.4225	4.5484	2.5468	7.0952
6	85.7483	4.4211	2.6742	7.0952
7	82.9405	4.2874	2.8078	7.0952
8	79.9923	4.1470	2.9482	7.0952
9	76.8966	3.9996	3.0957	7.0952
10	73.6462	3.8448	3.2504	7.0952
11	70.2333	3.6823	3.4129	7.0952
12	66.6497	3.5116	3.5836	7.0952
13	62.6462	3.3325	3.7627	7.0952
14	58.9361	3.1443	3.9509	7.0952
15	54.7876	2.9468	4.1485	7.0952
16	50.4317	2.7394	4.3559	7.0952
17	45.8581	2.5216	4.5736	7.0952
18	41.0557	2.2929	4.8024	7.0952
19	36.0133	2.0528	5.0424	7.0952
20	30.7187	1.8006	5.2946	7.0952
21	25.1594	1.5359	5.5593	7.0952
22	19.3221	1.2580	5.8373	7.0952
23	13.1930	.9661	6.1291	7.0952
24	6.7574	.6596	6.4356	7.0952
25	0.0000	.3379	6.7574	7.0952
		$77.3800	$100.0000	$177.3800

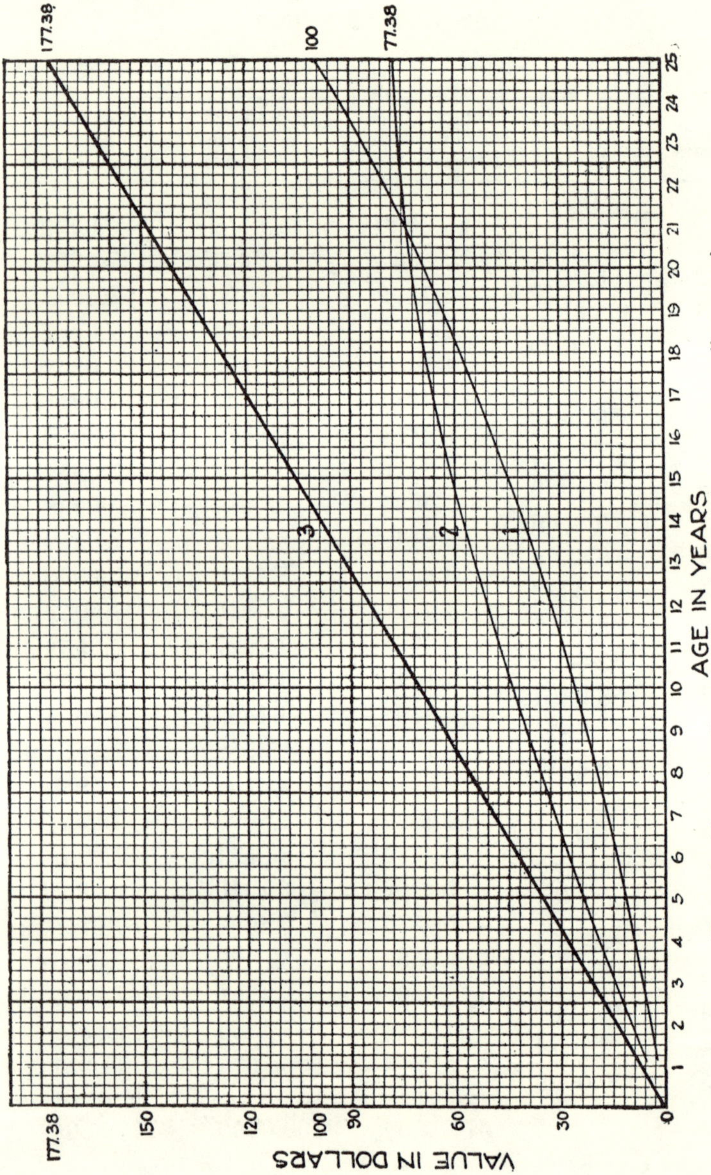

Form 8. Annuity Curves (plotted from data on preceding page)

CHAPTER XV

THE EQUAL ANNUAL PAYMENT METHOD

Characteristics

This method[1] has been devised for the purpose of securing an equalized depreciation charge, and thus a uniform investment cost. By investment cost is meant that part of the cost of the output which arises from the investment in the industrial plant, without which operations could not be carried on. Investment cost will depend upon the amount of capital sunk in the enterprise and the rapidity with which it is exhausted. Thus, if a plant capable of turning out one thousand units of a uniform product each year for 10 years, costs $10,000, then the investment cost per unit is $1, ignoring interest. If the $10,000 invested in the plant is worth 6% interest, then the total investment cost is $10,000 plus the interest on that amount for 10 years at 6%, or $16,000. This assumes that the total investment remains in the plant. If at the end of each year a portion of the investment is returned, as it should be under a proper system of charging for depreciation or exhausted capital outlay, the interest charge on the remaining investment will decrease each year in proportion to the amount of the investment so amortized, and the interest plus the investment will be considerably less than $16,000.

In theory this equal annual investment charge would be secured when, taking into consideration the interest cost on the continually decreasing investment, an equal annual charge is made against revenue that will cover both depre-

[1] Suggested by the Special Committee on Valuation of the American Society of Civil Engineers, in their tentative report of Dec. 31, 1913.

ciation of the remaining investment and the interest cost incident to such investment.

Assume the case of a property costing $100, having a lifetime of 25 years. The money invested has been borrowed at 5% interest. To simplify matters we shall for the present neglect salvage value and repairs. How can we determine the equal annual investment cost and therefore the annual depreciation charges to cover such cost, so that out of such charges the investment can be amortized and interest at 5% paid on the continually reducing investment? That is, instead of waiting until the end of the 25th year to repay the loan of $100, a payment is to be made thereon each year of a sum representing depreciation during the year plus interest on the investment as at the beginning of the year. The reduction of the interest charge will depend on the rapidity with which the investment theoretically depreciates and is amortized through the annual charges. Since interest cost gradually diminishes, it follows that to make the charge equal from year to year the depreciation must correspondingly increase.

Illustration of Equal Annual Payment Method

The sum which must be placed in a sinking fund each year so that such annual payments plus their accumulations at 5% compound interest will amount in 25 years to $100, is, according to the formula explained in Chapter XIII, $2.0952+. By the equal annual payment method, instead of establishing a sinking fund, each annual depreciation charge is made equal to what the annual payment to a sinking fund plus the interest accumulations for that year would have amounted to had such a fund been established. In the third column of the table which follows, the depreciation for each year is assumed to be equal to the annual increase of a sinking fund into which annual payments of $2.0952+

are made and allowed to accumulate at 5% interest, thus amounting to $100 at the end of 25 years. These amounts, when deducted from the amount invested as at the beginning of each year, give the remaining investment upon which interest for the next year is computed. The return on the remaining investment as at the beginning of each year is shown in the fourth column at 5%, and in the fifth column at 7%. The sixth and seventh columns show the depreciation and interest on the remaining investment combined. It is only when the same rate of interest is assumed for computation of the depreciation by the sinking fund method and for the interest on the remaining investment, that the amount of the two when combined remains a constant quantity.

Since a sinking fund is not really established, the following question arises: What is to determine the rate of interest to be employed in making the computation of the depreciation? This leads to a consideration of what appears to be the leading defect of the method, viz., that the amount of the depreciation, and consequently the amount of the remaining investment, is assumed to be dependent upon the laws of compound interest. There is no ground whatever for such an assumption, and if property depreciates to the same extent that a sinking fund accumulates, it is due merely to a coincidence, and one which it is safe to say never occurs in reality. This, however, does not necessarily negative the value of the plan, which, it would appear, might—after a careful comparison of the various sinking fund curves with actual conditions, to find what one most nearly approximates such conditions—be of much value in determining a uniform or nearly uniform charge.

Equal Annual Payment Tabulations

In the table which follows are given all the tabulations

Equal Annual Payment Method

TABLE OF COMPUTATIONS

Age in Years	Value at End of Year	Depreciation During Year	Return on Remaining Value of Property at: 5%	Return on Remaining Value of Property at: 7%	Combined Depreciation and Return Upon Investment at: 5%	Combined Depreciation and Return Upon Investment at: 7%
0	$100.0000					
		$2.0952	$5.0000	$7.0000	$7.0952	$9.0952
1	97.9048					
		2.2001	4.8952	6.8533	7.0953	9.0534
2	95.7047					
		2.3100	4.7852	6.6993	7.0952	9.0093
3	93.3947					
		2.4254	4.6697	6.5376	7.0951	8.9630
4	90.9693					
		2.5468	4.5484	6.3679	7.0953	8.9146
5	88.4225					
		2.6742	4.4211	6.1896	7.0953	8.8638
6	85.7483					
		2.8078	4.2874	6.0024	7.0952	8.8102
7	82.9405					
		2.9482	4.1470	5.8058	7.0952	8.7540
8	79.9923					
		3.0957	3.9996	5.5995	7.0953	8.6952
9	76.8966					
		3.2504	3.8448	5.3828	7.0952	8.6332
10	73.6462					
		3.4129	3.6823	5.1552	7.0952	8.5681
11	70.2333					
		3.5836	3.5116	4.9163	7.0952	8.4999
12	66.6497					
		3.7627	3.3325	4.6655	7.0952	8.4282
13	62.8870					
		3.9509	3.1442	4.4021	7.0952	8.3530

Equal Annual Payment Method (*Continued*)

TABLE OF COMPUTATIONS

Age in Years	Value at End of Year	Depreciation During Year	Return on Remaining Value of Property at:		Combined Depreciation and Return Upon Investment at:	
			5%	7%	5%	7%
14	58.9361					
15	54.7876	4.1485	2.9468	4.1255	7.0953	8.2740
16	50.4317	4.3559	2.7394	3.8351	7.0953	8.1910
17	45.8581	4.5736	2.5216	3.5302	7.0952	8.1038
18	41.0557	4.8024	2.2929	3.2101	7.0953	8.0125
19	36.0133	5.0424	2.0528	2.8739	7.0952	7.9163
20	30.7187	5.2946	1.8006	2.5209	7.0952	7.8155
21	25.1594	5.5593	1.5359	2.1503	7.0952	7.7096
22	19.3221	5.8373	1.2580	1.7612	7.0953	7.5985
23	13.1930	6.1291	.9661	1.3525	7.0952	7.4816
24	6.7574	6.4356	.6596	.9235	7.0952	7.3591
25	0.0000	6.7574	.3379	.4730	7.0953	7.2304
		$100.0000	$77.3800	$108.3300	$177.3800	$208.3300

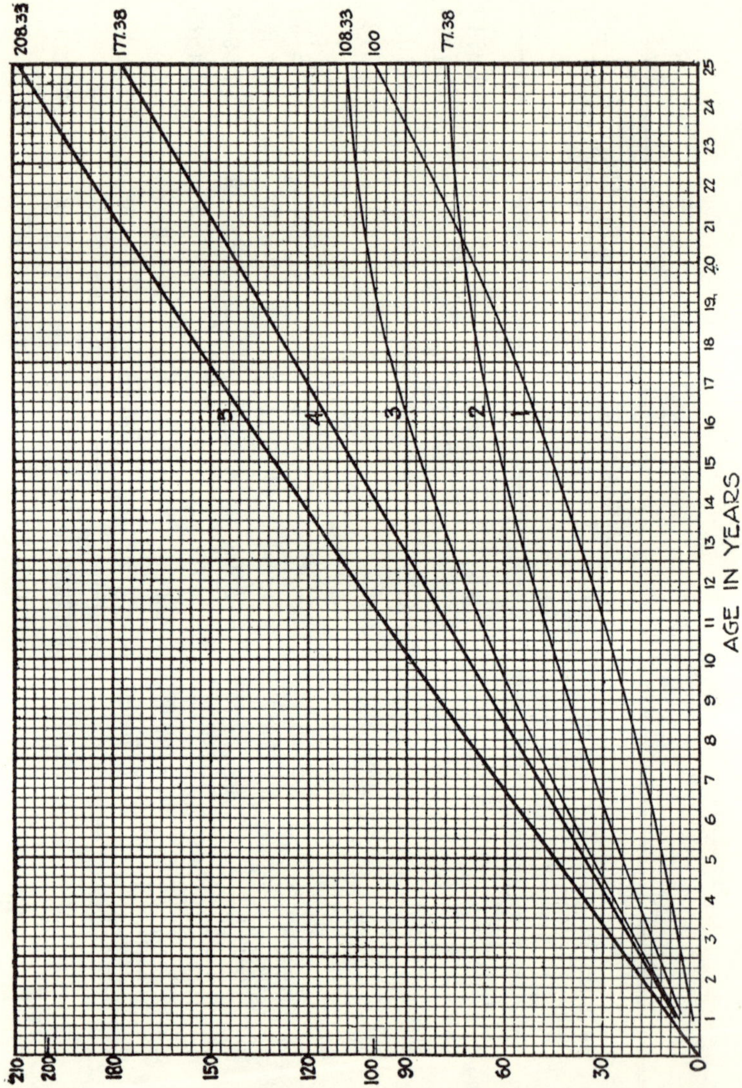

Form 9. Curves Illustrating Equal Annual Payment Method (plotted from data on pages 162, 163). The figures at left of curves indicate value in dollars.

illustrative of this plan for an investment of $100, having a lifetime of 25 years, with depreciation based on a sinking fund accumulating at 5% compound interest, and returns of 5% and 7%, respectively, on the remaining investment. The items in the sixth column are formed by combining the items of the third and fourth columns; while the items in the seventh column are formed by combining the items of the third and fifth columns.

Graphic Illustration of Equal Annual Payment Method

In Form 9 these facts are indicated graphically. Curve 1 represents depreciation; curve 2 represents return on the investment at 5%; curve 3 represents return on the investment at 7%. The straight line 4 is the resultant of curves 1 and 2, while curve 5 represents the resultant of 1 and 3. Note that while 4 is a straight line, 5 is slightly curved, owing to the slightly decreasing charge, as shown in the seventh column of the table.

CHAPTER XVI

THE UNIT COST METHOD

Characteristics

This is a modification of the sinking fund method, based, its advocates claim, on the proposition that decrease of plant value is determined by increased cost of service or output, and may result either from obsolescence or actual physical depletion. It is claimed by the advocates of the unit cost method that the sinking fund formula is not of a sufficiently general type to take into consideration all the factors which enter into the problem; as, for example, the loss in economy resulting from the use of an old machine. The unit cost method, it is said, takes into consideration these factors, being based on the principle that the true price of a second-hand machine is such that during its remaining life the cost of output will be the same as during the life of a new machine.

The Unit Cost Formula

The unit cost formula is developed on the basis of value applicable to a given depreciated machine, and on value applicable to a new machine. That is, by making a comparison of a worn and a new plant on the basis of known or assumed facts, their relative values are found to be such that a unit of output will cost the same for the old as for the new machine. To accomplish such a result it is necessary to take into consideration the following factors: (1) the cost of amortizing the new machine; (2) the depreciated value of the old machine; (3) the average annual operating expenses, not including repairs, of both machines for their given lifetime; (4) the annuities which will be sufficient to provide repairs for both machines; and (5) the number of units of output which each machine is capable of producing. These values, for use in developing the unit cost formula, may be expressed as follows:

V = first cost of new machine.
v = depreciated value of old machine.
F = sinking fund annuity to amortize V in its life of N years.
f = sinking fund annuity to amortize v in its life of n years.
N = lifetime in years of new machine.
n = remaining lifetime in years of old machine.
Q = average annual operating expense of new machine, not including repairs, during N years.
q = average annual operating expense of old machine, not including repairs, during remaining lifetime of n years.
P = annuity necessary to meet repairs of new machine during N years.
p = annuity necessary to meet repairs of old machine during n years.
i = rate of interest.
U = average cost per unit of output of new machine for N years.
u = average cost per unit of output of old machine for n years.
Y = average number of units of output per annum of new machine during N years.
y = average number of units of output per annum of old machine during n years.

The average unit cost for the old and new machines may be expressed thus:

$$(1) \qquad U = \frac{Q + P + F + iV}{Y}$$

$$(2) \qquad u = \frac{q + p + f + iv}{y}$$

According to our theorem, the unit cost of both old and new machines must be the same; therefore:

$$(3) \qquad \frac{Q + P + F + iV}{Y} = \frac{q + p + f + iv}{y}$$

According to formula (4) in Chapter XIII, the V being dropped as it here equals 1, the sinking fund annuity necessary to accumulate \$1 in N years is:

$$(4) \qquad X = \frac{(r - 1)}{(r^N - 1)}$$

Substituting $(1 + i)$ for r we have:

$$(5) \qquad X = \frac{i}{(1 + i)^N - 1}$$

Similarly the sinking fund annuity necessary to accumulate \$1 in n years is:

$$(6) \qquad x = \frac{i}{(1 + i)^n - 1}$$

To accumulate V dollars in N years will therefore require an annuity of:

$$(7) \qquad F = XV = \frac{iV}{(1 + i)^N - 1}$$

To accumulate v dollars in n years will require an annuity of:

$$(8) \qquad f = xv = \frac{iv}{(1+i)^n - 1}$$

These values of F and f may now be substituted in equation (3), as follows:

$$(9) \qquad \frac{Q + P + XV + iV}{Y} = \frac{q + p + xv + iv}{y}$$

Equation (9) may now be solved for v, the depreciated value of the old plant. Multiplying both terms by y,

$$(10) \qquad q + p + xv + iv = y\,\frac{(Q + P + XV + iV)}{Y}$$

Transferring $(q + p)$ to the opposite side by changing their sign,

$$(11) \qquad xv + iv = y\,\frac{(Q + P + XV + iV)}{Y} - (q + p)$$

Since v is common to both items of the left-hand side of the equation, it may be written:

$$(12) \qquad v(x + i) = y\,\frac{(Q + P + XV + iV)}{Y} - (q + p)$$

Dividing both terms of the equation by $(x + i)$ we have:

$$(13) \quad v = \frac{y}{(x + i)} \times \frac{(Q + P + XV + iV)}{Y} - \frac{(q + p)}{(x + i)}$$

Or, extending the parentheses to include $(q+p)$ by multiplying and dividing it by $\frac{y}{(x+i)}$ (thus leaving its value unchanged), we have:

$$(14) \quad v = \frac{y}{x+i}\left(\frac{Q+P+XV+iV}{Y} - \frac{q+p}{y}\right)$$

which is the general form of the unit cost formula. Values of X and x are calculated by the sinking fund formulas (5) and (6).

If the annual number of units of output of the old and new machines are the same, then $Y=y$ and equation (14) becomes:

$$(15) \quad v = \frac{(Q+P+XV+iV-q-p)}{(x+i)}$$

Or,

$$(16) \quad v = \frac{V(X+i)+(Q+P-q-p)}{(x+i)}$$

When the average annual operating expenses of the old and new plants are the same, $Q=q$ and the formula becomes:

$$(17) \qquad v = \frac{V(X+i)+(P-p)}{(x+i)}$$

When $Q+P=q+p$, the formula becomes:

$$(18) \qquad v = \frac{V(X+i)}{(x+i)}$$

which may be proven to be but another form of the sinking fund formula.

Illustration of Unit Cost Method

Let \$100 represent the cost of a unit of plant, with an estimated lifetime of 25 years, 5 years of which has expired. Let 5% be the rate of interest on the investment, while the average annual operating expense, excluding repairs, is \$50 a year. The annuity to provide for repairs during the remaining years is \$12. When this plant unit was purchased it was clearly worth its full cost. With the passage of time, however, improvements are made, so that a machine of equal durability may be secured 5 years later at a cost of \$100, which will turn out an average of 40 units per annum, at a reduction from \$12 to \$11 per annum for repairs, and from \$50 to \$48 for operating expense. Interest on investment remains the same. It is estimated that the old machine will turn out, on an average, 38 units per annum during the rest of its lifetime, 20 years.

If now we substitute these values in formula (14), we have:

$$v = \frac{38}{.03024 + .05}\left(\frac{\$48 + \$11 + \$2.0952 + \$5}{40} - \frac{\$50 + \$12}{38}\right)$$

From this we find the value of v—which is the depreciated value of the old plant—to be \$9.85.

The accuracy of the results secured by this method are commented on in Chapter X.

Appendix

CHAPTER XVII

LOGARITHMS AND THEIR USE

Computing Interest

Interest computations extending over long periods, as well as other calculations involving extended processes of multiplication and division, or the finding of powers and roots, are greatly facilitated by the use of logarithms. When, for example, it is necessary to compute the amount of an annuity, i.e., of a series of equal annual payments, of, let us say, $10 each, for a period of 30 years, accumulating at a rate of 6% compound interest, the work of doing this by the usual arithmetical process is exceedingly laborious. Thus, the computations for the first three years are as follows:

First annual payment........................	$10.00
	× 1.06
	6000
	1000
Amount at end of 1st year..................	$10.60
Add 2nd annual payment.....................	10.00
Principal at beginning of 2nd year..........	$20.60
	× 1.06
	12360
	2060
Amount at end of 2nd year.................	$21.836

Amount at end of 2nd year (brought forward)	$21.836
Add 3rd annual payment....................	10.00
Principal at beginning of 3rd year...........	$31.836
	× 1.06
	191016
	31836
Amount at end of 3rd year..................	$33.74616

One can readily see that to carry this on for the full 30 years would be a burdensome task. Hence a shorter method is desirable. It will be noted that the amount of the fund at the end of each year is obtained by multiplying it by the ratio of increase, 1.06, which gives the same result as is secured by first finding the interest by multiplying the principal at the beginning of each year by .06, and then adding this to the principal to find the amount at the end of the year. Therefore, if we wish to find the amount of $10 when placed at compound interest at 6% for 30 years, our work will be abbreviated by first multiplying 1 by 1.06 thirty times, and then finding the product of $10 multiplied by the result, which may be expressed thus:

$$\$10 \times 1.06^{30}$$

In case of an annuity of $10 for 30 years the problem is somewhat more complicated, because there is not merely one sum of $10 accumulating at compound interest, but a series of annual instalments of that amount, each drawing interest. In a 30-year period, if the first of the 30 annuities is paid at the beginning of the first year, it will have a period of 30 years during which to accumulate. The last instalment will be paid at the beginning of the 30th or last year, and each one will draw interest; but since the last one has only one year during which it will accumulate, its interest is not compounded.

On the other hand, if the first of the 30 annuities is paid at the end of the first year, it will have not 30, but 29 years during which to accumulate, and the last annuity, being paid at the end of the 30th year, accumulates no interest at all. This is an important distinction, and, as depreciation allowances for the year must be made as of the end of the year and not at the beginning—for the depreciation accrued during the year—calculations must in such a case be based on the fact that the last annuity bears no interest and the first one bears interest from the end of the first, or, what amounts to the same thing, from the beginning of the second year. This must be kept in mind in the discussion of the sinking fund formula in Chapter XIII.

Assuming, then, that the first of the annuities or instalments of $10 each, begins to accumulate interest at the end of the first year, at 6%, it is evident that it will accumulate interest for 29 years, and will amount to:

$$\$10 \times 1.06^{29}$$

Similarly the next annuity will accumulate to:

$$\$10 \times 1.06^{28}$$

and so on, until we come to the next to the last instalment, which will accumulate to:

$$\$10 \times 1.06$$

and the last one, which will have no time to accumulate any interest whatever. Briefly, each annuity accumulates to 1.06 times the amount to which the one immediately following accumulates. Thus we have a series of amounts, increasing or decreasing by a common ratio, depending upon which way we view it, exactly the same as the series discussed in Chapter XIII, whose sum, V, is expressed by the following formula:

$$V = x \frac{(r^n - 1)}{(r - 1)}$$

in which x is the annuity, r is 1 plus the rate of interest, and n the number of years. Therefore the accumulations, at compound interest, of an annuity of $10, for 30 years at 6%, the first annuity being paid at the end of the first year, is expressed thus:

$$10 \frac{(1.06^{30} - 1)}{1.06 - 1}$$

Principle of Logarithms

A short method of making the computation indicated by 1.06^{30}, which is read as 1.06 raised to the 30th power, or simply as 1.06 to the 30th power, will be found in the use of logarithms. To understand this use a study of the underlying principle upon which logarithms are based will be necessary.

We can raise any number to any desired power by multiplying itself by itself the required number of times; thus 2^3 means $2 \times 2 \times 2$, or 8; 3^4 means $3 \times 3 \times 3 \times 3$, or 81; 4^4 means $4 \times 4 \times 4 \times 4$, or 256, and so on. From what has just been said the following is self-evident.

3	to	1st	power	is	3
3	"	2nd	"	"	9
3	"	3rd	"	"	27
3	"	4th	"	"	81
3	"	5th	"	"	243
3	"	6th	"	"	729
3	"	7th	"	"	2187
3	"	8th	"	"	6561
3	"	9th	"	"	19683
3	"	10th	"	"	59049

and so on. The numbers in the second column are the indices, indicating the power to which 3 is raised to secure the number in the third column. Thus, $3^9 = 19683$; $3^5 = 243$.

Now suppose that we desire to multiply 243 by 81. By ordinary multiplication, $243 \times 81 = 19683$. From the foregoing table it may be seen that $243 = 3^5$, and $81 = 3^4$. By a principle of mathematics known as the law of indices, $3^5 \times 3^4 = 3^{5+4} = 3^9$. That is, 3^5 is multiplied by 3^4 by simply adding together the indices. That this is correct may be seen by a glance at the table. There we find that 3^9 equals 19683, as we have already found by multiplication. Conversely, $243 \div 81 = 3^5 \div 3^4 = 3^{5-4} = 3^1 = 3$; for 3 raised to the 5th power is 243, and this amount, 243, divided by 3^4, or 81, gives 3. Thus, in a very simple way, we have substituted addition and subtraction for multiplication and division.

Let us suppose further that we desire to extract the square root of 59049. As will be seen from the table, this is 3 raised to the 10th power, or 3^{10}. The square root of 59049 is therefore the same as the square root of 3^{10}. According to the law of indices, dividing the index of a number by 2 is equivalent to extracting the square root. Therefore, $3^{\frac{10}{2}}$, or 3^5, is the square root of 3^{10}. According to our table $3^5 = 243$. That this is the square root of 59049 may be seen by multiplying 243 by 243, which equals 59049. By reversing the procedure a number may be raised to any power by simply multiplying its index by that power. Thus 243, or 3^5, may be squared by multiplying 5, the index of 3, by 2; thus $243^2 = 3^{5 \times 2} = 3^{10} = 59049$. Similarly $27^3 = 3^{3 \times 3} = 3^9 = 19683$.

The Logarithm

In the table given on page 175, the numbers in the second

column are said to be the logarithms of the numbers in the third column to the base 3. In other words, the logarithm of a number is the power to which its base must be raised to produce that number. Thus, 8 is the logarithm of 6561 to the base 3, and 2 is the logarithm of 9 to the base 3.

We have here selected the number 3 as a base. Any number may be so employed. The number 10 is the base usually taken, and forms the basis of the common system of logarithms.[1] Therefore common logarithms of numbers are indices indicating the power to which 10 must be raised to equal those numbers, just as in our table they were indices of 3.

Since most numbers are not integral powers of 10, it follows that their logarithms are integers only in the rare cases that they are integral powers of 10. Thus, $10^2 = 100$; therefore 2 is the logarithm of 100 to the base 10. Similarly 3 is the logarithm of 1000 to the base 10, and 4 is the logarithm of 10000 to the base 10. But the logarithm of 500 must be something more than 2 and less than 3; that is, it is 2 plus a decimal. A five-place logarithm table gives this decimal part of the logarithm to five points, as........
.... .69897
A six-place table gives it as..... .698970
A thirteen-place table gives it as.. .6989700043360
A twenty-place table gives it as.. .69897000433601880479

Usually the last figure is not exactly correct, being approximated or rounded off just as we round off $18.217 to $18.22.

The Characteristic

The integral part of a logarithm is known as the char-

[1] Any good table of common logarithms such as those appearing in mathematical textbooks may be referred to in connection with the problems presented in this volume.

acteristic of the logarithm. Thus the logarithm of 500 to the sixth place is 2.698970, and therefore the characteristic of the logarithm of 500 is 2. Similarly the characteristic of the logarithms of all numbers from 100 to 999, inclusive, is 2; for the logarithm of 100 is 2, the logarithm of 999 is 2.999565, and the logarithms of all numbers between 100 and 999 lie between 2 and 2.999565.

The logarithm of 1000 is 3, for $10^3 = 1000$. The logarithm of 9999 is 3.999957. Therefore the characteristic of the logarithms of all numbers from 1000 to 9999 is 3, and so on. It will be noted that the characteristic of any logarithm is determined by the position of the decimal point in its number, being independent of the digits of the number. Thus, the characteristic of the logarithm of 7, which has one unit figure, is zero; of the logarithm of 77.77, which has one figure to the left of the unit place, is 1; of the logarithm of 9.3, with one unit figure, is 0; of the logarithm of 3742.17, with three figures to the left of the unit place, is 3; of the logarithm of 56689.778, with five figures to the left of the unit place, is 4; and so on. Hence, to find the characteristic of the logarithm of a number, this rule is given:

To find the characteristic of the logarithm of a number, find how many places the first significant figure is removed from unit's place. This determines the characteristic, and it is positive or negative (plus or minus) accordingly as the first significant figure is to the left or right of unit's place. Thus:

Characteristic of the logarithm of	1.	is 0
" " " " "	0.1	" $\bar{1}$ (minus 1)
" " " " "	22.0	" 1
" " " " "	.0222	" $\bar{2}$
" " " " "	275.0	" 2
" " " " "	.0004	" $\bar{4}$
" " " " "	1785.27968	" 3

The Mantissa

The mantissa of the logarithm of a number is the decimal portion, and does not depend upon the location of the decimal point but upon the digits of which the number is composed. Thus, while the characteristics of the logarithms of 999, 99.9 and 9.99 are 2, 1, and 0, respectively, the mantissa is the same for all, viz., .999565. Again, the characteristic of the logarithms of 327, 729, and 211 is 2 in each case, but the mantissas are .514548, .862728, and .324282. While the characteristic is positive or negative, depending upon the position of the decimal point, the mantissa is always positive. The mantissa is found by the use of a table of logarithms.

Finding the Logarithm of a Number

The number being given, its logarithm is determined by first finding the characteristic by the rule given. The mantissa is found from a table of logarithms, as follows:

1. When the number is composed of not more than four figures:

In the first column of the table of logarithms find the first two or three or four figures of the number (according to the table used), then follow across on the same line until the column is reached headed by the same figure as the last digit in the number whose logarithm we wish to find.[2] The decimal so found is the mantissa. To avoid repetition in the table, the first two (sometimes three or four) figures of the mantissa are printed at intervals only, in the second column.

Find log 37.53. By the rule the characteristic is 1. In the first column of the table of logarithms, find 375, and on the same line in the column headed by last digit 3, is found

[2] A six-place table is employed in the computations which follow.

the mantissa .574379. As the characteristic is 1, the logarithm of 37.53 is 1.574379. Similarly:

Log 727.4............2.861773
Log 3256. ....3.512684
Log 7274.0............3.861773

2. When the number is composed of more than four figures:

By glancing at the table of logarithms it will be seen that, within certain limitations, the numbers are proportional to their logarithms, and *vice versa.* Thus:

Log 4290....3.632457	} difference is .000102	
" 4291....3.632559	} " " .000101	
" 4292....3.632660	} " " .000101	
" 4293....3.632761		

Thus, while the difference between the numbers is constantly 1, the difference between the logarithms is nearly constant. These differences, 102, 101, and 101, are known as the *tabular differences,*[3] and their almost constant amount corresponds in a very close degree to the difference of unity between the numbers. The logarithms are therefore nearly proportional to their corresponding numbers, and may be assumed to be exactly proportional to them for practical purposes. Consequently, if any one of the numbers be increased by 0.1, its corresponding logarithm will be increased by .1 of the tabular difference between the logarithm of that number and the logarithm of the next higher number. Thus:

Log 4290.1 = 3.632467 (or 3.632457 + .1 of 102)

[3] In practice the ciphers preceding the difference figures in the mantissas are disregarded to save time and space, but care must be taken in the interpolation process to add the differences in their proper places to the right of the decimal point.

Log 4290.2 = 3.632477 (or 3.632457 + .2 of 102)
" 4290.9 = 3.632549 (or 3.632457 + .9 of 102)

This process of finding logarithms of numbers between two numbers in the table is called interpolation. To lessen the work, in some tables the tabular differences are inserted in a separate column, and at the bottom of the page is sometimes given the proportional part of the last figure. Thus, if the tabular difference is 102, the additions to be made for .1, .2, .3, .4, and so on, are 10, 20, 31, 41, and so on. Had the number whose logarithm was to be found been 42901 instead of 4290.1, the mantissa would have been the same, but the characteristic would have been 4 instead of 3.

If the number is composed of six figures, as 429015, and a five-place table is used, the correction for the last two figures is found by interpolation as indicated above. The correction for the fifth figure is .1 of 102, or 10, and the correction for sixth figure is .05 of 102, or 5; hence 15 must be added to 3.632457, the logarithm of 4290, which gives 5.362472 for the logarithm of 429015.

Finding the Number Corresponding to a Logarithm

Given the logarithm of a number, the number itself may be discovered by the use of a table of logarithms. First, from the characteristic of the logarithm the position of the decimal point is determined, the operation being simply the reverse of that employed in finding the characteristic. Thus, if the characteristic is always the same as the number of places the first significant figure is removed from unit's place, it follows that in the number corresponding to a given logarithm the number of places the first significant figure is removed from unit's place will depend upon the characteristic, being to the left or right of unit's place accordingly as the characteristic is positive or negative.

Now if the mantissa appears in the table, the corresponding number is found immediately. Thus, to find the number whose logarithm is 2.791059, we find, by reference to a table of logarithms, that the corresponding number is 618.1, the position of the decimal point being determined as noted above.

If, however, no mantissa is found in the tables in exact agreement with the mantissa whose number we wish to find, the first four figures of the mantissa are found, and then by the principle of proportional parts additional figures can be added. Thus, to find the number whose logarithm is 1.325220, we turn to the table and find that this mantissa lies between .325105 and .325310. We now proceed as follows:

Mantissa of log of	2115	=	.325310
" " " "	2114	=	.325105
Differences	1		205

Mantissa of log of required number		=	.325220
" " " "	2114	=	.325105
Differences	(?)		115

By the principle of proportional parts,

$$(?) : 1 :: 115 : 205$$

$$\text{or} \quad (?) = \frac{115}{205} = .5609+$$

the figures which must be annexed to 2114 to give the number whose logarithm is 1.325220. Thus the required number is 21.145609+, the decimal point being determined by the characteristic, which is 1. Beyond the first three additional figures obtained by interpolation, their accuracy cannot be depended on, so that the sixth place is the last one to be retained. Instead of using the phrase, "number whose logarithm is 1.32522," the following briefer expression, "$\log^{-1}$ 1.32522," is commonly employed. Thus:

$$\text{Log}^{-1}\ 2.75631 = 570.571$$
$$\text{Log}^{-1}\ .00352 = 1.00814$$

Finding Powers and Roots of Numbers

In the first part of this chapter we have seen the necessity of a convenient method of finding high powers of numbers in making interest computations. Thus, an annuity of $10, at 6% compound interest, amounts in 30 years to:

$$10\ \frac{(1.06^{30} - 1)}{1.06 - 1}$$

The reduction of this rather complex form necessitates the raising of 1.06 to the 30th power, which is an extremely tedious process by multiplication. Since the multiplication of the logarithm of a number by a given number has the same effect as raising that number to the power indicated by the given number, the following process should be carefully studied:

$$\text{Log}\ 1.06 = .025306$$
$$.025306 \times 30 = .759180$$
$$\text{Log}^{-1}\ .759180 = 5.74354$$

which is the 30th power of 1.06.

In the same way that any desired power of a number may be found by multiplying its logarithm by the number representing the desired power and then finding the number in the table corresponding to the logarithm represented by the product, so any desired root of a number may be found by dividing the logarithm of that number by the number indicating the root to be found, and then finding the number in the table whose logarithm is the quotient.

Find the 30th root of 5.74354.

$$\text{Log } 5.74354 = .759179$$
$$.759179 \div 30 = .0253059$$
$$\text{Log}^{-1}\ .0253059 = 1.06$$

which is the 30th root of 5.74354.

Referring again to the problem in hand, and substituting 5.74354 in:

$$10 \cdot \frac{(1.06^{30} - 1)}{1.06 - 1}$$

we find its value to be $790.59, the amount of the annuity of $10, at 6% compound interest, for 30 years.

CHAPTER XVIII

SELECTED BIBLIOGRAPHY

The references given herewith are only to such books and articles as it is believed will be most useful to the student making a general study of the subject of depreciation. A very complete bibliography may be found in volume 76 of the Transactions of the American Society of Civil Engineers, pages 2133-2193; also in Whitten's Valuation of Public Service Corporations, pages 735-745.

Books

Dicksee, L. R. Depreciation, Reserves, and Reserve Funds. 80 pages. London, 1912.

Floy, Henry. Valuation of Public Utility Properties. 390 pages. New York, 1912.

Humphreys, A. C. Lecture Notes on Some of the Business Features of Engineering Practice. 565 pages. Hoboken, N. J., 1912.

Matheson, Ewing. The Depreciation of Factories. 230 pages. London, 1910.

Leake, P. D. Depreciation and Wasting Assets. 195 pages. London, 1912.

Whitten, R. H. Valuation of Public Service Corporations. 798 pages. New York, 1912.

Articles

Alvord, John W. The Depreciation of Public Utility Properties as Affecting Their Valuation and Fair Return. Proceedings American Society of Civil Engineers, Nov., 1913, pages 2045-2060. Claims that depreciation should be deducted for rate-making purposes, unless represented by a definite sinking fund.

Britton, John A. Depreciation. Progressive Age, June 15, 1908, Vol. 26, page 379. Cites several court decisions substantiating the inclusion of depreciation as an operating expense.

Chase, Harvey S. Maintenance and Depreciation Charges in Accounts of Public Service Corporations. Journal of Accountancy, May, 1907, Vol. 4.

Cooley, M. E. Factors Determining a Reasonable Charge for Public Utility Service. Journal of Western Society of Engineers, Jan., 1914, pages 1-17.

Duffy, C. N. Depreciation. Electric World, Feb. 1, 1908. Gives details on electric power plants, classifies specific assets, and suggests methods of handling depreciation. Applies to Wisconsin conditions. See editorial in same paper. Same article in Progressive Age, Sept. 1, 1909.

Depreciation Allowance for Income Tax (England). Journal of Gas Lighting, Nov. 23, 1909, Vol. 108, pages 517, 518.

Delano, Frederick A. Application of a Depreciation Charge in Railway Accounting. Journal of Political Economy, Nov., 1908, Vol. 16, pages 585-601.

Geijsbeek, J. B. Fair Return to Public Utilities. Journal of Accountancy, Vol. 17, April, 1914.

Gillette, H. P. Use of Depreciation Data in Rate Making. Electrical World, Nov. 2, 1912.

Gray, Henry L. Necessity of Depreciation Reserves. Railway Age Gazette, May 27, 1910, page 1297.

Grunsky, C. E. The Appraisal of Public Service Properties as a Basis for the Regulation of Rates. Transactions of the American Society of Civil Engineers, Vol. 75, page 770. Maintains that depreciation should not be deducted for rate-making purposes, but that original investment should be used for fixing rates, on the theory that the investment must be maintained intact; first, by the maintenance of the plant, and, second, by a sum set aside for renewals from time to time.

Humphreys, A. C. Depreciation. Progressive Age, Dec. 2, 1907, Vol. 25, pages 688-699. A criticism of the valuation work of the "sō-called experts."

Humphreys, A. C. Depreciation, Estimated and Actual. Proceedings of the American Gas Institute, 1913, Part 2, pages 505-530.

Jackson, W. B. The Depreciation Problem. Annals of the American Academy of Political and Social Science, Jan., 1911.

Knight, Alfred. Depreciation and Other Reserves. Journal of Accountancy, Jan., 1908, Vol. 5, pages 189-204.

Mack, Edwin S. Depreciation. Progressive Age, June 15, 1908, Vol. 26, pages 372-375.

Neal, J. H. Where Maintenance Ends and Depreciation Begins. Proceedings of American Street and Interurban Railway Accountant's Association, 1907, Vol. 2, pages 195-202.

Obsolescence of Electric Lighting Plant. Electrical Review (London), Sept. 25, 1908, Vol. 63, pages 516, 517.

Prouty, Charles A. The Work Involved in the Valuation of Railroads. Railway Age Gazette, Feb. 13, 1914, Vol. 56, pages 320-323.

Riggs, H. E. Valuation of Public Service Corporations Property. Proceedings of the American Society of Civil Engineers, Nov., 1910.

Staub, Walter A. Deferred Charges to Operating. Journal of Accountancy, Oct., 1909, Vol. 8, pages 401-418.

Stockwell, H. G. Depreciation Renewal and Replacement Accounts. Journal of Accountancy, Dec., 1909, and Jan., 1910, Vol. 9, pages 87-103, 189-210.

Treatment of Depreciation in Connection with the Federal Corporation Tax. Journal of Accountancy, March, 1912, pages 218-222.

Wilmot, H. W. Depreciation. Journal of Accountancy, Dec., 1909, Vol. 9, pages 104-113.

Wilgus, W. J. Appraisal of the Lehigh Valley Railroad. Engineering Record, May 30, 1914, Vol. 69, pages 613-617. Compiled from directions issued by Mr. Wilgus for the guidance of his staff in the appraisal of the Lehigh Valley Railroad.

INDEX

C

W

DIMENSIONS OF ACCOUNTING THEORY AND PRACTICE

An Arno Press Collection

The American Association of University Instructors in Accounting. **Papers and Proceedings of the American Association of University Instructors in Accounting.** 1916-1925

Baily, Francis. **The Doctrine of Interest and Annuities.** 1808

Beckett, Thomas. **The Accountant's Assistant.** 1901

Blough, Carman G. **Practical Applications of Accounting Standards.** 1957

Bray, F[rank] Sewell. **Precision and Design in Accountancy.** 1947

Brief, Richard P., editor. **Dicksee's Contribution to Accounting Theory and Practice.** 1980

Brinton, Willard C. **Graphic Methods For Presenting Facts.** 1914

Brooks, Collin, editor. **The Royal Mail Case.** 1933

Burns, Thomas J. and Edward N. Coffman, editors. **Ohio State Institute of Accounting Conferences: Collected Papers, 1938-1963.** 1980

By a Chartered Accountant and William A. Vawter Foundation on Business Ethics. **The Etiquette of the Accountancy Profession and The Ethical Problems of Modern Accountancy.** 1927/1933

Carey, John L. **Professional Ethics of Public Accounting.** 1946

Cerboni, Giuseppe. **Primi Saggi Di Logismografia Presentati All' XI Congresso Degli Scienziati Italiani In Roma.** 1873

Cleveland, Frederick A. **Chapters on Municipal Administration and Accounting.** 1909

Cocke, Sir Hugh. **A Summary of the Principal Legal Decisions Affecting Auditors.** 1946

Cotter, Arundel. **Fool's Profits.** 1940

Courcelle-Seneuil, J.G. **Traité Élémentaire de Comptabilité.** 1869

Daniels, Mortimer B. **Corporation Financial Statements.** 1934

DeMond, C.W. **Price, Waterhouse & Company in America.** 1951

Devine, Carl Thomas. **Inventory Valuation and Periodic Income.** 1942

Dicksee, Lawrence Robert. **Business Methods and the War** with **The Fundamentals of Manufacturing Costs;** and **Published Balance Sheets and Window Dressing.** 1916/1927, 1928

Dicksee, Lawrence Robert. **Business Organisation.** 1910

Dicksee, Lawrence Robert and Editor of the Accountant's Library. **Fraudulent Accounting** and **Fraud in Accounts.** 1909/1924, 1925

Edwards, J.R., editor. **British Company Legislation and Company Accounts, 1844-1976.** 1980

Ficker, Nicholas Thiel. **Shop Expense.** 1917

Goldberg, Louis. **An Inquiry Into the Nature of Accounting.** 1965

Green, David, Jr. **Accounting for Corporate Retained Earnings.** 1980

Greene, Catharine De Motte. **The Dynamic Balance Sheet.** 1980

Hain, Hans Peter. **Uniformity and Diversity.** 1980

Hawawini, Gabriel A., and Ashok Vora, editors. **The History of Interest Approximations.** 1980

Hepworth, Samuel Richard. **Reporting Foreign Operations.** 1956

The Herwood Library of Accountancy. 1938

The Institute of Chartered Accountants in England and Wales *Library Catalogue, 1913.* 1913

The Institute of Chartered Accountants in England and Wales **Library Catalogue, 1937.** 1937

Het Internationaal Accountantscongres, Amsterdam 1926. 1927

Johnson, H. Thomas, editor. **System and Profits: Early Management Accounting at DuPont and General Motors.** 1980

King, George. **The Theory of Finance.** 1882

Langenderfer, Harold Q. **The Federal Income Tax: 1861-1872.** 1980

Leake, P.D. **Commercial Goodwill.** 1921

Leautey, Eugene and Adolfe Guilbaut. **La Science Des Comptes Mise A La Portée De Tous.** 1889

Levy, Saul. **Accountants' Legal Responsibility.** 1954

Lubell, Myron Samuel. **The Significance of Organizational Conflict on the Legislative Evolution of the Accounting Profession in the United States.** 1980

Marchi, Francesco. **I Cinquecontisti.** 1867

Merino, Barbara, editor. **Business Income and Price Levels.** 1980

Norris, Harry. **Accounting Theory.** 1946

O'Neill, Michael T., editor. **A.P. Richardson: The Ethics of a Humanist.** 1980

Parker, R.H., editor. **Bibliographies for Accounting Historians.** 1980

Parker, R.H., editor. **British Accountants: A Biographical Sourcebook.** 1980

Perera, M.H.B. **Accounting for State Industrial and Commercial Enterprises in a Developing Country.** 1980

Previts, Gary John. **A Critical Evaluation of Comparative Financial Accounting Thought in America 1900 to 1920.** 1980

Rich, Wiley Daniel. **Legal Responsibilities and Rights of Public Accountants.** 1935

Richardson, A[lphyon] P[erry], editor. **The Influence of Accountants' Certificates on Commercial Credit.** 1913

Roberts, Alfred R., editor. **Selected Papers of Earle C. King.** 1980

Saliers, Earl A. **Principles of Depreciation.** 1915

Schiff, Michael, editor. **The Hayden Stone Accounting Forums 1962-1967.** 1980

Schmalenbach, Eugen. **Dynamic Accounting.** 1959

Scovell, Clinton H. **Cost Accounting and Burden Application.** 1916

Sprague, T[homas] B[ond]. **A Treatis on Life Insurance Accounts** and **A Treatise on Insurance Companies' Accounts** 1874/1911

Stacey, Nicholas A.H., **English Accountancy 1800-1954.** 1954

Stamp, Edward, G.W. Dean, and P.W. Wolnizer, editors. **Notable Financial Causes Célèbres.** 1980

Staubus, George J. **An Accounting Concept of Revenue.** 1980

Taylor, R. Emmett. **No Royal Road.** 1942

Todhunter, Ralph. **Institute of Actuaries' Text-Book of the Principles of Interest, Life Annuities, and Assurances, and Their Practical Application.** 1901

Wells, Murry C., editor. **Controversies on the Theory of the Firm, Overhead Allocation and Transfer Pricing.** 1980

Wildman, John R. and Weldon Powell. **Capital Stock Without Par Value.** 1928